ARVO PÄRT'S
Tabula Rasa

Oxford KEYNOTES
Series Editor KEVIN C. KARNES

Sergei Prokofiev's Alexander Nevsky
KEVIN BARTIG

Rodgers and Hammerstein's Carousel
TIM CARTER

Aaron Copland's Appalachian Spring
ANNEGRET FAUSER

Arlen and Harburg's Over the Rainbow
WALTER FRISCH

Beethoven's Symphony No. 9
ALEXANDER REHDING

Arvo Pärt's Tabula Rasa
KEVIN C. KARNES

Oxford KEYNOTES

ARVO PÄRT'S
Tabula Rasa

KEVIN C. KARNES

Oxford University Press is a department of the University of Oxford. It furthers
the University's objective of excellence in research, scholarship, and education
by publishing worldwide. Oxford is a registered trade mark of Oxford University
Press in the UK and certain other countries.

Published in the United States of America by Oxford University Press
198 Madison Avenue, New York, NY 10016, United States of America.

© Oxford University Press 2017

All rights reserved. No part of this publication may be reproduced, stored in
a retrieval system, or transmitted, in any form or by any means, without the
prior permission in writing of Oxford University Press, or as expressly permitted
by law, by license, or under terms agreed with the appropriate reproduction
rights organization. Inquiries concerning reproduction outside the scope of the
above should be sent to the Rights Department, Oxford University Press, at the
address above.

You must not circulate this work in any other form
and you must impose this same condition on any acquirer.

Library of Congress Cataloging-in-Publication Data
Names: Karnes, Kevin, 1972– author.
Title: Arvo Pärt's Tabula rasa / Kevin C. Karnes.
Description: New York : Oxford University Press, 2017. |
Series: Oxford keynotes | Includes bibliographical references and index.
Identifiers: LCCN 2017005341 | ISBN 9780190468989 (pbk. : alk. paper) |
ISBN 9780190468972 (hardcover : alk. paper)
Subjects: LCSH: Pärt, Arvo. Tabula rasa.
Classification: LCC ML410.P1755 K36 2017 | DDC 784.2/72—dc23
LC record available at https://lccn.loc.gov/2017005341

Series Editor's INTRODUCTION

OXFORD KEYNOTES REIMAGINES THE canons of Western music for the twenty-first century. With each of its volumes dedicated to a single composition or album, the series provides an informed, critical, and provocative companion to music as artwork and experience. Books in the series explore how works of music have engaged listeners, performers, artists, and others through history and in the present. They illuminate the roles of musicians and musics in shaping Western cultures and societies, and they seek to spark discussion of ongoing transitions in contemporary musical landscapes. Each approaches its key work in a unique way, tailored to the distinct opportunities that the work presents. Targeted at performers, curious listeners, and advanced undergraduates, volumes in the series are written by expert and engaging voices in their fields, and will therefore be of significant interest to scholars and critics as well.

In selecting titles for the series, Oxford Keynotes balances two ways of defining the canons of Western music: as lists of works that critics and scholars deem to have articulated key moments in the history of the art, and as lists of works that comprise the bulk of what consumers listen to, purchase, and perform today. Often, the two lists intersect, but the overlap is imperfect. While not neglecting the first, Oxford Keynotes gives considerable weight to the second. It confronts the musicological canon with the living repertoire of performance and recording in classical, popular, jazz, and other idioms. And it seeks to expand that living repertoire through the latest musicological research.

Kevin C. Karnes
Emory University

CONTENTS

ABOUT THE COMPANION WEBSITE   *viii*
ACKNOWLEDGMENTS   *ix*
ARCHIVES AND SOURCES   *xi*

1. The Blank Slate   *1*
2. Unofficial Music: A History for Pärt   *17*
3. *Tintinnabuli*   *37*
4. *Tabula Rasa*: Listening, Reading   *61*
5. Export and Emigration   *95*

ADDITIONAL SOURCES FOR READING AND LISTENING   *113*
NOTES   *115*
INDEX   *131*

ABOUT THE COMPANION WEBSITE

Oxford University Press has created a website to accompany *Arvo Pärt's Tabula Rasa* that features a variety of related multimedia materials, including audio clips for all in-text musical examples. Many of these resources are integral to the volume itself or provide needed and useful context. As with all of the websites for Oxford Keynotes volumes, the reader is encouraged to take advantage of this valuable online information to expand their experience beyond the print book in hand. Examples available online are indicated in the text with Oxford's symbol ⏵.

www.oup.com/us/aptr
Username: Music2
Password: Book4416

The reader is invited to explore the full catalog of Oxford Keynotes volumes on the series homepage.
www.oup.com/us/oxfordkeynotes

ACKNOWLEDGMENTS

My work on this project was inspired, assisted, and enabled by many. In Atlanta, students in my Emory University seminar on Pärt in the spring of 2014 were an incredible source of ideas and conversation, as have been my friends and colleagues John Lysaker and Stephen Crist. Emory College of Arts and Sciences provided funds for travel and a sabbatical year in which to write. Emory College and Emory's Laney Graduate School of Arts and Sciences supported the work of my expert research assistant, Jordan Daniels.

It was at a festival and conference in Canterbury in 2011 that I began thinking seriously about writing on Pärt's music, largely in response to conversing and listening with Jeffers Engelhardt and Tina K. Ramnarine. I am grateful to Tina, Jeffers, and Christopher J. May for reading drafts of this book as it took shape, and likewise to the anonymous manuscript reviewers for Oxford University Press. I am indebted to Chris, Kevin Bartig, Lisa Jakelski, and Peter Schmelz for helping track down some elusive sources, and to Don Giller for preparing the musical examples.

In Estonia my research has been nurtured at every turn, by some whom I have known for years and others I met only recently: Urve Lippus, Toomas Siitan, and Anu Kõlar at the Estonian Academy of Music and Theatre; Kristiina Kiis at the Estonian Theatre and Music Museum; Gerli Rebane at the Film Archives of the Estonian National Archive; and the staff of the radio archives of Estonian Public Broadcasting. I am especially grateful for the support and assistance of Arvo and Nora Pärt, and for the help of the unbelievably generous staff of the Arvo Pärt Centre in Laulasmaa, especially Kristina Kõrver and Kai Kutman. Thank you.

ARCHIVES AND SOURCES

A<small>LL RARE OR PREVIOUSLY</small> unpublished material described, quoted, or included in this book is cited according to the archive in which the documents or items are preserved, along with identifying catalog numbers where applicable. In many cases, I describe or quote from newspaper articles preserved as clippings bundled in folders, sometimes without identifying information. In all cases I have attempted to provide full citations for the materials to which I refer, but where information has proven elusive I cite the archive and location of the clipping in question. All translations from original documents in Russian, German, French, Latvian, and other languages are my own, but where previously published translations are available I reference those as well. I have prepared translations from documents in Estonian with considerable help from Jeffers Engelhardt, and in Finnish with help from Tina K. Ramnarine. The following abbreviations are used in the endnotes:

APC	Arvo Pärt Centre, Laulasmaa, Estonia
EFA	Estonian Film Archives (Eesti Filmiarhiiv), Tallinn

EPB	Estonian Public Broadcasting (Eesti Rahvusringhääling), Tallinn
ETMM	Estonian Theatre and Music Museum (Eesti Teatri- ja Muusikamuuseum), Tallinn
Gespräch	*Arvo Pärt im Gespräch*, ed. Enzo Restagno (Vienna: Universal Edition, 2010)
Conversation	*Arvo Pärt in Conversation*, ed. Enzo Restagno, trans. Robert Crow (Champaign, IL: Dalkey Archive Press, 2012)

ARVO PÄRT'S
Tabula Rasa

CHAPTER 1
THE BLANK SLATE

"I COULD COMPARE MY music to white light, in which all colors are contained. Only a prism can separate the colors from each other and make them visible. This prism could be the spirit of the listener." In the liner notes to his 1995 album *Alina*, Arvo Pärt compared his music to the blank slate of brilliant, full-spectrum luminescence, a tabula rasa upon which to inscribe—or maybe find illuminated—one's own stories and imaginings, experiences, and longings.[1] Pärt's words on his music are deeply evocative, but on their own they do little to distinguish it from many other musics that resounded across Europe and North America in the 1990s. After all, the ability of music to accommodate a seemingly limitless range of engagements, responses, and projections by listeners has been widely acknowledged for years.[2] Perhaps more remarkable about Pärt's work is something that might seem to be the opposite of his point: the relatively narrow range of images that typically attend accounts of his music, and *Tabula Rasa* particularly—his concerto for two violins, amplified prepared piano, and orchestra composed in 1977. Time and again those accounts trade in tropes of stillness and timelessness, ritual and healing.

Pärt's music, writes the conductor Paul Hillier, "ushers us into the presence of a recurring process: for ritual is not simply the repetition or reenactment of structured events, but rather a return to a perennial condition."[3] Pärt himself, the singer Björk observed, seems to be a figure with "the whole battle of this [twentieth] century inside him."[4] For the critic Alex Ross, Pärt's work has the effect of "obliterat[ing] the rigidities of space and time" and "binding the mind to an eternal present."[5] Describing his work in an AIDS clinic in the 1980s ("despondent months, when even AZT was still an experimental drug"), the critic Patrick Giles reported that "some of us discovered not a treatment, but at least a balm: a 1977 album of music by an Estonian classical composer with the peculiar name Arvo Pärt." That album, he recalled, "brought comfort to many of us after we'd given up on the very possibility of it."[6] Revisiting Giles's account in 2002, Ross confided: "several people have told me essentially this same story about the still, sad music of Pärt—how it became, for them or for others, a vehicle of solace. One or two such anecdotes seem sentimental; a series of them begins to suggest a slightly uncanny phenomenon."[7]

Part of the project of this book is to take a close look at observations like these, to ask what there is about *Tabula*

Rasa and Pärt's other "tintinnabuli" compositions that prompts these kinds of reflections on timelessness and healing among so many listeners. Another part of the project will be to ask where such tropes might have come from in the first place, and to inquire about the ways in which they have served to situate the composer and his music amidst the far-flung communities and spaces they have inhabited. These include the imaginary spaces traversed by those who experience Pärt's music through mediated pathways for creativity and encounter, spaces shaped by figures like Björk and Hillier, by Ross's readers and Giles's friends in the clinic, and also by countless listeners to Pärt's recordings and users of social media. Those spaces also include the historical locales of the Soviet Union in the 1970s, where *Tabula Rasa* was composed and premiered; West Germany and Austria, where Pärt found an early audience and settled after leaving the USSR in 1980; and the transitional spaces of the "New Europe" (and North America) of the 1980s and '90s, where the very notion of a Europe divided was being reconsidered, and where Pärt and his music offered focal points and soundtracks for imagining and configuring a post–Cold War world.

Ranging broadly across these histories and spaces, the thesis of this book is this: *Tabula Rasa* bears and has borne, since its earliest imaginings, the indelible imprint of Pärt himself, and also of all the individuals and groups that enabled its composition and premiere, as well as all the others who have subsequently performed it, attended its soundings, produced its recordings, acquired its records, shared their understandings, listened again, and made *Tabula Rasa* their own. This might seem like an obvious point to make about any work of music. But it is crucial with respect to a work by Pärt, who, perhaps more than any other living composer, has borne what can seem the unshakable burden of a way of thinking about composers' lives that is deeply rooted in a kind of romantic historicism still common in discourse on famous musicians.[8] To this romantic way of thinking, Pärt seems a solitary, even heroic figure, who struggled through trials and isolation to find his creative voice, whose music was initially met with incomprehension and hostility, and who fled from oppressive political circumstances to find freedom—both political and musical—in the democratic West. All of these statements are true to a point. But the problem with regarding Pärt in this way, without taking account of all the other circumstances and people who helped shape his history, is that it encourages a mythologizing of his life and work and uncritical ways of thinking about both. If we accept this romantic narrative at face value, then Pärt's published words and official biography might seem to tell us all there is to know about his art.[9] And the stylistic contours of his music—quiet, sparse, deliberate, austere—might seem in turn to provide a mirror of the composer's inner and outer lives. All too easily, the composer, like his music, can become a tabula rasa upon which to project our own imaginings of whomever we might wish him and ourselves to be. This book is an attempt to demythologize one corner of Pärt's history and work: his discovery and early experiments with *tintinnabuli*, and tabula rasa in particular.

As the musicologist Oliver Kautny began to document years ago, a romanticized view of Pärt began to crystallize even before he emigrated from his native Estonia, then a

Soviet republic.[10] In an interview from 2001, the Russian violinist Tatiana Grindenko, who with Gidon Kremer commissioned *Tabula Rasa*, recalled her first impressions of Pärt at a festival of new music held in Riga in 1976. In her account, Pärt was an artist who cut a typically romantic figure: a recluse who found his creative voice while toiling in isolation from the broader world. In Pärt, she remembered, she met a man "who rejected [everything] and lives in the country," who seemed as though he "came out of the underground for the first time" bearing the first traces of his new *tintinnabuli* style.[11] Another romantic archetype was conjured in some of the earliest press Pärt received abroad: the struggling hero, with his heroism rooted in his supposed dissidence with respect to Soviet authorities. Almost always, such assertions were grounded in social or artistic connections that Pärt himself played little role in forging. In 1978, in the politically sensitive aftermath of the defection of the Soviet conductor Kirill Kondrashin, the BBC Symphony canceled a planned London performance of Pärt's *Cantus in Memory of Benjamin Britten* (1977), a move that prompted the *Guardian* to proclaim: "there are dissident Soviet composers too."[12] The following year, the West German city of Cologne hosted a festival called "Encounters with the Soviet Union," which Soviet authorities criticized sharply for having been organized without their involvement. Among the compositions programmed at the festival were several by Pärt, all of which were performed, a German paper reported, in such a way that "sent wafting upward the fine incense of dissident art."[13]

After leaving Estonia in 1980 and settling first in Vienna and then in West Berlin, other romantic portrayals took

FIGURE 1.1 "L'énigme Arvo Pärt," *Le monde de la musique*, October 1987, p. 69.

hold. With his signature black beard and Orthodox Christian faith, Pärt was described as a "mystical enigma" and an "eccentric saint" in the press of Paris and New York (figure 1.1).[14] In a statement on his art that he penned for a volume of 1990 called *Soviet Music in Light of Perestroika*, Pärt described his work as consisting in "flight into voluntary poverty." He explained his metaphor with reference to his creative turn of the 1970s, from the complexities of serial composition toward the simpler lines and triads of *tintinnabuli*. But in a book on music and perestroika compiled in the thick of Gorbachev's reforms, it was hard to avoid reading his words in relation to his more recent and literal flight from the USSR, with the cost of the journey having been registered in the everyday struggles—often heroic, to be sure—faced by all such immigrants and their families in those years.[15] What all of these observations and statements have in common is that they make Pärt into a figure upon which we can easily hitch our own imaginings: of renegade composers, Soviet trials, and the promise of the Cold War West.

It is important as well to recall that the world from which Pärt had come when he landed in Vienna was still a blank slate for many people living and listening in geographically and politically Western spaces. In the spring of 1981, just as he was settling in Berlin after a stay and naturalization in Austria, a special issue of the *Neue Zeitschrift für Musik*, West Germany's leading music magazine, was dedicated to perspectives on musics in and of the USSR. Eliding the empire with its largest republic, the journal's editor opened the issue by observing how striking it was that "Russia, as a musical continent, has remained *terra incognita* up to the present day."[16] It was just five hundred miles from Kaliningrad to Berlin and a stone's throw over the Berlin Wall to Moscow's nearest satellite state. But the editor regarded the Soviet Union as a world apart and away, a vast blank space on the cultural map of postwar Europe.

As it happened, Pärt's arrival in the divided city coincided almost exactly with the first, tentative beginnings—emblematized in that same special issue of the *Neue Zeitschrift für Musik*—of what would soon become a momentous opening of the Cold War East to the gaze and imaginings of a curious and searching West. In 1983 and '84 the Czech novelist Milan Kundera burst into the mainstream of Western commentary with a series of essays published in France, England, and the United States highlighting moments and conditions of cultural community and shared historical experience that transcended geopolitical divisions. His goal was to challenge the very premise of reflexively dividing Europe into Eastern and Western domains.[17] In 1986 the British journalist Timothy Garton Ash went so far as to ask whether "Central Europe"—that ubiquitous and notoriously ambiguous moniker for an elusive middle ground, culturally Western but politically Eastern, possibly extending from East Berlin all the way to Pärt's native Estonia—existed at all as a meaningful marker on the cartography of the contemporary European imagination.[18] On MTV, glimmers of a hopeful turn were given emblematic voice by Sting, who ventured from his band, the Police, to assure his listeners, with the peculiar mix of wariness and optimism that characterized much of the eastward gazing of these years, that nuclear war will never transpire because "the Russians love their children too" ("Russians," 1985). This came just a year after another British act, Frankie Goes to Hollywood, mocked the posturing of Cold War antinomies with its dramatic video "Two Tribes" (1984).

Amid this swell of questioning and reimagining the political, historical, and emotional landscapes of past, present, and future Europe, Pärt broke into the mediated imagination of Western spaces with the 1984 release of his first album with ECM Records in Munich, entitled *Tabula Rasa*. The violinist Gidon Kremer, who helped commission the namesake composition and soloed on two of the album's four tracks, later recalled that the disc "became a sort of cult record [*Kultplatte*] for many, from the world of popular music as well."[19] With this crossover success, at once commercial and artistic, Pärt and his music became widely recognizable points of reference on the blank slate of a continent that suddenly seemed in the midst of uncertain transition. He was a figure whose history, music, and dwelling-places—whose languages, faith, and even physical appearance—planted him squarely on the immanently movable, possibly untenable, and perhaps even fading line between East and West.

In the 1990s, after the fall of the Berlin Wall and the end of the Soviet Union as a political entity, a new wave of gazing eastward washed over classical music circles in North America and Britain, as concerts and recordings made unlikely celebrities of Pärt and Henryk Górecki, a contemporary composer from Poland. (Górecki's Symphony No. 3, in an artfully designed and expertly marketed Nonesuch CD of 1992, became a historic bestseller in classical and crossover markets.) Together, the two were widely treated as exponents of an ostensible movement dubbed "holy" or "mystical minimalism."[20] Minimalism referred broadly to a way of thinking and composing associated foremost with the Americans Steve Reich and Philip Glass, who sought alternatives in the 1960s and '70s to the structural complexities and modernist visions of the American, West German, and Italian avant-garde. (In fact, I will suggest that Pärt's *tintinnabuli* owes a great deal to the very tendencies the minimalists rejected.) Mystical referred in part to the Christian texts set in some of Pärt's and Górecki's works. But it stood more broadly for qualities of timelessness or stasis widely ascribed to their music by listeners. As the *Guardian* cheekily sought to clarify in a piece on "holy minimalism" from 1992, "How can you spot it? Pious subject matter, harmonic stasis and snail-like progress (aka 'time suspended')."[21] That stasis was often heard in relation to the composers' supposed aspirations to a particular kind of transcendence: specifically, to transcendence of the weight of modern Europe's violent, materialistic, ideological past. "It aspires to a suspension of time and history," wrote Edward Rothstein in the *New York Times*, "offering a much needed, [if] only temporary comfort, a beguiling taste of religious faith."[22] For one writer, the holy minimalists sought escape from histories inscribed by idealist traditions of Western philosophy, which had fueled the spirit of twentieth-century revolutions and had supposedly found musical embodiment in the dramatic gestures of Beethoven's symphonies.[23] For the musicologist David Clarke, the past that these composers sought to transcend was embodied instead in elite artistic modernism, where, in Theodor Adorno's famous formulation, the atonal music of Arnold Schoenberg had unmasked and reflected the psychologies and social structuring that culminated in the catastrophe of World War II.[24]

This discourse on holy minimalism was sparked first and foremost by the success of Pärt and Górecki in the marketplace, a success that the discourse itself helped to stoke and maintain in turn. But it borrowed its terms and visions from another, vital conversation of these years, about the recently inaugurated and presumably final chapter of Europe's twentieth-century history. For some, the collapse of European communism seemed to signal "not just the end of the Cold War, or the passing of a particular period of postwar history, but the end of history as such," as the American philosopher Francis Fukuyama proclaimed triumphantly in 1989.[25] Namely, it foretold the imminent transcendence of those historical forces—perhaps born of romantic idealism, possibly reflected in avant-garde modernism—that had given rise to the unprecedented disasters of the twentieth century. As Alex Ross wrote of Pärt and other "mystical minimalists" in 1993, they seemed to compose "as if the history of music were at an end."[26] And just as Fukuyama had pointed to the end of European communism as foretelling and cementing history's end, so too a writer for the *Guardian* regarded that same political turn as portending the rise of holy minimalism in music. "Something had to happen of course," wrote the journalist Edward Pearce of postwar modernism. "The avant garde was a little like communism: media power, contempt for non-party members, a gullible intelligentsia and . . . a distinct police regime saying what should be exalted, what not heard." Yet now, Pearce observed, that modernism had finally "run out of credit . . . [and] could function only so long before, in its Brezhnev phase, browning over. But escape has not come through alternative diktat. The market has settled this one."[27]

Clarke and Rothstein were more skeptical than this. All such visions of history's end, they argued, were utopian, even dangerous. But to revisit the discourse on holy minimalism that all of these writers helped to shape reminds us of how profoundly such longings to transcend the weight of a divisive past inflected discussions of Pärt's work just as it was becoming known by many. Its popular discovery took place in a time when a Europe long divided seemed finally on a path toward healing, and to purging its memory of the historical forces that had rent it in the first place. For some, Pärt's music seemed to offer a soundtrack for that longed-for mending, a sounding experience of the tranquil, resonant harmony to be attained after escape from history's debilitating course. This discourse echoed the tropes of timelessness and healing considered at the start of this chapter, but on a scale that was continental, even world historical. Here Pärt's work was cast as music for the end of history itself, and for the new, posthistorical Europe poised to rise from the ashes.

From within this hazy discourse on Pärt, his music, and their worlds, this book will attempt a sober examination of his discovery and early experiments with *tintinnabuli*, and of the sounds of *Tabula Rasa*. Before embarking on this project, however, we should linger for just a moment longer on another variety of healing glimpsed in discourse on the composer from within the spaces he left behind when he departed Estonia in 1980. For what can we make of a line of writing in late and formerly Soviet spaces that emphasizes continuity over discontinuity in Pärt's biography and the evolution of his music? Unlike many writers in England, Germany, and the United States, who regard Pärt's *tintinnabuli* as a radical break from his earlier work, the Estonian musicologist Uno Soomere heard Pärt's first *tintinnabuli* compositions as "continuing along the lines" of his earlier music, in terms of the "considerable weight" the composer gives to "every sound, line, and coloring."[28] And whereas Hillier regards *tintinnabuli* as "one of the forces displacing the hitherto central language of serialism" in the "contemporary musical world,"[29] the Russian musicologist Svetlana Savenko located the technical roots of *tintinnabuli* squarely within the sounds and concerns of Pärt's own serial compositions of the 1960s. "If he disowns serialism," Savenko wrote in October 1991,

> Pärt nonetheless builds on [*razvivaet*] some of its important elements. To a considerable extent, the strictness and rationalism of [his] motivic techniques, architectonic construction, and calculating approach to composition are indebted to the serialist discipline of his earlier work. It is as if Pärt is transferring the idea of serialism onto modal material, and the total diatonic style of *tintinnabuli* turns out to be the flip side of the total chromatic of serialism, its dialectical opposite, its "antiphonal echo."[30]

Speaking in West Berlin in 1987, Pärt confided that it was difficult for him to believe he was the same person who had composed his early serial works. "The things I create now," he averred, "and those from before are opposites, but it is a fact that they came from the same place. It's difficult for me to say anything about that today."[31] But in the autumn of 1991, as the USSR was clearly disintegrating and its institutions were falling into disarray and uncertainty, and in what would be one of the final issues of the once-exalted journal *Sovetskaia muzyka*, Savenko held that Pärt was presently indebted, in the very deepest of ways, to his formative experiences of serial composition within the socialist state. In 2005 she repeated her argument, essentially unchanged.[32]

By that year, the midpoint of the second decade of the post-Soviet era, Pärt and his music were being welcomed back warmly to Estonia, the place he had left a quarter of a century ago, now an independent republic again.[33] In Savenko's writing, Pärt was being reclaimed for even broader spaces of historical memory and present habitation.

For although Pärt's serialist experience "of much earlier times" might have been "decisively repudiated by the composer," Savenko claimed that his *tintinnabuli* works still bore the indelible, formative imprint of a great musical culture that survived in memory, if not quite literally on the concert stages of a reimagined Europe. In Pärt's music, her words suggest, one still hears echoes of a vital past, when Estonians and Russians were undivided by the borders reinstated after 1991. On the pages of even Pärt's newest scores one still finds traces of the music of the Soviet avant-garde, forged in a time when musicians were united by a sense of excitement born of sometimes subversive curiosity. Listening to Pärt as Savenko does, we too might hear echoes of a historical world that is easily forgotten today, of a place and an age of trials and limitations that was also—as one of Pärt's Estonian friends recalled in 1999—"a very good time for art."[34] With the profoundly dislocating events of 1989–91, an empire was fragmented and its inhabitants were rent from its living history in innumerable and very tangible ways. To heal those rifts, to ameliorate that loss, was yet another task assigned to Pärt and his *tintinnabuli* music.

The rest of this book will trace and mine some of the histories glimpsed above. We will begin in Soviet spaces: the avant-garde circles of Pärt's twenties and thirties, with the individuals and institutions that made his music alternately celebrated and unplayable. I will then detail Pärt's discovery of the ideas and structures he describes as *tintinnabuli*, and I will consider how that discovery transformed and also left untouched the ways in which his music was constructed and sounds. Next, I will turn to *Tabula Rasa* directly, listening carefully and reading closely for continuities and disruptions while trying simultaneously to render its sounds comprehensible in one way or another. Finally, I will examine the circumstances of the work's export and Pärt's emigration, the mediation of his music after the experience of the USSR, and some of the affordances that *Tabula Rasa* has offered to those who have listened and created in its wake.

CHAPTER 2

UNOFFICIAL MUSIC
A HISTORY FOR PÄRT

P<small>ÄRT'S RELATION TO HIS</small> history in the USSR is understandably fraught. Recently he declared through a spokesman that the whole of "the period of the Soviet Union" was "a completely closed chapter" for him, one "he is not prepared to evoke" again.[1] But *Tabula Rasa* was composed and premiered in Soviet spaces and he discovered *tintinnabuli* while working in the capital of the Estonian SSR, so it is important to confront and explore these histories if we wish to understand how the sounds of his music came to be. A useful construct we might adapt to these ends is that of "unofficial music," elaborated by the musicologist Peter Schmelz to describe works and events of the 1950s and '60s that were neither officially sanctioned nor explicitly opposed by Soviet authorities.[2] After the death of Stalin in 1953 and Nikita Khrushchev's consolidation of power three years later, cultural life in the Soviet Union saw a newfound openness to artistic experiments and an influx of artworks from abroad. In this climate, a handful of young composers began to mine the musics of the twentieth-century West, from the twelve-tone works of Arnold Schoenberg to the "total serialism" of Pierre Boulez and the indeterminacy of John Cage, for models and inspiration in their own creative searching. Among that handful was Pärt, who entered Tallinn Conservatory in 1957 and graduated six years later.

As it had been since the 1930s, "official" music of the period remained locked within the uncertain confines of Soviet socialist realism, as promoted by often nameless officialdom and policed by the Ministry of Culture and the Union of Soviet Composers. Such music was to be broadly accessible in terms of its tonal and melodic language, and it was to affirm, in its subjects and texts, sanctioned political ideology and the greatness or promise of the Soviet state or peoples.[3] In contrast, unofficial music was often esoteric in terms of its construction, and it usually avoided sanctioned themes. Whereas official music was purchased by the state, performed under the auspices of philharmonics (regional organizations responsible for official concert programming), and published by government-run firms, unofficial music typically premiered in composers' residences, private clubs, or university lecture halls, and it often remained unpublished, generating no income for its composers. A phenomenon that confounds the simple dissidence-versus-compliance binary that framed a great deal of Cold

War discourse, unofficial music was not a manifestation of dissent—or even, necessarily, of protest. It simply stood outside the system of state-controlled musical patronage. Over the course of the 1950s and '60s, when Pärt was studying and establishing a career, institutional attitudes toward unofficial music were anything but stable. Pärt was alternately celebrated and condemned for the unofficial music he composed. But he wrote official music as well, and his experiences in both realms left indelible marks upon what would become his *tintinnabuli* style.

As Schmelz documents, the relative openness of the 1950s and '60s was itself a foundational experience, maybe *the* foundational experience, in the creative lives of many composers of Pärt's generation, including Andrei Volkonsky, Sofia Gubaidulina, and Alfred Schnittke. Visits by Igor Stravinsky, the pianist Glenn Gould, and the Italian composer Luigi Nono afforded previously inaccessible glimpses of early twentieth-century modernism and the postwar Western avant-garde. Scores of such music began circulating privately. Even the official journal *Sovetskaia muzyka* published on Schoenberg's twelve-tone system, if only to disparage it officially. By the start of the 1960s, as Schmelz puts it, "all of the 'young composers'"—Pärt, Gubaidulina, and the rest—"realized that they had been denied important aspects of their musical education" in their conservatory training.[4] The works and curricula they studied formally constituted only a small and seemingly uninteresting slice of the expansive field of musical possibilities their glimpses of the West now afforded. As early as 1956–57 Volkonsky had composed a piano piece called *Musica Stricta*, based on the idea and sound—if not a detailed understanding—of

Schoenberg's dodecaphony. Widely regarded as the first such composition by a postwar Soviet artist, *Musica Stricta* elicited condemnation in no less exalted a forum than the Twenty-second Congress of the Communist Party, held in October 1961. The following March, Tikhon Khrennikov, longtime chair of the Composers' Union, issued a warning to other young artists about the perils of following Volkonsky's lead. The warning came too late for Pärt, however, for in that very statement Khrennikov singled out Pärt's dodecaphonic *Nekrolog* (1960) for attack.[5]

For a composer who had yet to receive his conservatory diploma, to be subjected to blistering criticism from the country's highest authority on music might have spelled the premature end of a career. But as Pärt recounted in the Parisian press a quarter of a century later, the uproar over *Nekrolog* seemed to have the opposite effect. Referring to an early performance of the work in Yugoslavia, he explained: "The scandal at the Zagreb festival was considerable.... I instantly became a celebrity. At the time, the lesser of the storms was political. But dodecaphony! In my view, that style of composing had more affinities with the communist system than with the capitalist one. But the censor was of a different mind."[6]

In fact, Pärt's words recall much of the noise in the system of Soviet bureaucracy in the Khrushchev years, which enabled and even contributed to the popular success of his work. As Kautny documents, when Pärt first presented *Nekrolog* to his colleagues at the Estonian branch of the Composers' Union in October 1960, he explained that it had been "composed in memory of those executed at Kalevi-Liiva"—a coastal site east of Tallinn where occupying Nazi forces murdered thousands of Estonian Jews and others during World War II. For many of his colleagues, upon whose approval Pärt depended if the work were to be performed in public, Pärt's project seemed to harness the dissonant sounds of Schoenberg's dodecaphony to a proper socialist realist project: recalling the catastrophe of World War II with a musical language plausibly apprehensible as an expression of radical violence (▶ audio 2.1).[7] With the Estonians' largely positive response as a prelude to official censure in Moscow, Pärt's work effectively opened a rift between the central authorities of Soviet bureaucracy and what some regarded as the more liberal environment of Pärt's home city of Tallinn. From that point forward, Pärt's music would be front and center in official discussions of unofficial music. As his work evolved over the course of the 1960s, so too did opinions and understandings about just where the boundary between official and unofficial music might lie.[8]

During these early years of his career, Pärt composed in deliberately official channels alongside unofficial ones. For two of his works in the former domain, *Our Garden*, for children's choir and orchestra (*Meie aed*, 1959), and the cantata *Stride of the World* (*Maailma samm*, 1961), he received top prize at an all-union showcase of music by young composers, just months after Khrennikov had excoriated him for *Nekrolog* (▶ audio 2.2).[9] But it was, in the end, his continuing work in sometimes unofficial realms that cemented Pärt's fame in Estonia and abroad. Between 1960 and 1968, as Toomas Siitan notes, each of Pärt's successive works seemed to encapsulate his encounter with a new or different avant-garde technique or gesture, from the approximate dodecaphony of *Nekrolog* to the stricter use of twelve-tone procedures in his Symphony No. 1 (1963), from aleatoric writing in *Diagrammid* for piano (1964) to quotation and multistylistic writing in *Collage über B–A–C–H* (1964).[10] Some of Pärt's works from this period exemplify distinctive ways of thinking and constructing musically that are clearly evident in *Tabula Rasa*, including a preoccupation with logical or algorithmic processes as means of generating pitch material or structures and an abiding concern for making those processes immediately apprehensible by listeners, however complicated the pitch constructions they generate might be.

We can get a sense of these facets of Pärt's early music by taking a look at a couple of scores, starting with the highly rational structure of *Perpetuum Mobile* for orchestra (1963). The basis for the work is the twelve-tone row shown in example 2.1.

EXAMPLE 2.1   Pärt, *Perpetuum Mobile*, twelve-tone row.

As Schoenberg's vision of dodecaphony prescribed some four decades earlier, Pärt's row comprises one statement each of all twelve pitches of the chromatic scale. To generate the pitch content of *Perpetuum Mobile*, Pärt has the orchestra play through the row six times, using all four of its possible permutations: in its basic (prime) form, backwards (retrograde), upside down (in inversion), and in retrograde inversion. Rather than having any single instrument perform the row as if it were a melody, Pärt assigns each of its pitches to a single instrument in the orchestra: the second violins play the B♭, the violas play the A, the third violins play the G♯, and so on. Each instrument's performance of its preassigned pitch overlaps with those played just before and after it, so that the opening B♭ is held under the A, the A is held under the G♯, and so forth. The overall effect is one of a gradual coalescence of an expanding cloud of dissonant pitch material and ever-shifting orchestral colors (▶ audio 2.3).

Possibly inspired by Boulez's attempts to subject every parameter of his music to serial procedures, Pärt superimposed his twelve-tone row upon a sequence of twelve durational values, so that each pitch in the row is played for a precisely predetermined length of time (example 2.2).[11]

EXAMPLE 2.2 *Perpetuum Mobile*, durational row.

The second violins play their B♭s as dotted whole notes, the violas play their As as whole notes, and so on. The row's durational values get steadily shorter from beginning to end, making the series sound increasingly frenetic as it unfolds: the opening pitches of the row are played in a slow and measured manner, and its final pitches are articulated quickly and repeatedly. The climax of *Perpetuum Mobile* arrives with the beginning of the orchestra's fifth pass through the row, which Pärt superimposes upon a retrograde version of the series of twelve durations—starting with sixteenth notes, then slowing to eighth notes, then slowing further to quarters. With this move, as the orchestra's fourth pass through the row nears its end, the frenetic pace of articulations is not relieved by a sudden return to longer note values. Rather, the orchestra careens full speed into the frantic start of the row's fifth sounding (▶ audio 2.4). All these gradual buildups, followed by a burst of quick pulsation two-thirds of the way through, have the effect of lending to the whole the quality of a wave or tremor, building slowly and then breaking into an explosion of cacophonous energy before dying down. The piece is one of Pärt's most rigorous experiments with the serial procedures approached in *Nekrolog*, presented in an intensely gripping, even viscerally moving way.

In another composition from these years, *Solfeggio* (1963), Pärt brought the rigidly systematic construction of *Perpetuum Mobile* to bear upon tonal or potentially tonal materials—as if to reveal, as Savenko wrote of *Tabula Rasa* and other *tintinnabuli* works, that a "diatonic style" can "turn out to be the flip side of the total chromatic of serialism."[12] Over its three-minute course, the choral *Solfeggio* unfolds much like *Perpetuum Mobile*. Once again, a predetermined row of pitches is performed repeatedly from beginning to end, with each pitch in the row sung by a different voice and with successively articulated pitches overlapping with those coming before and afterward. But unlike *Perpetuum Mobile*, the row in *Solfeggio* is not dodecaphonic. Rather, it consists of the seven diatonic pitches of the ascending C major scale (example 2.3, ▶ audio 2.5).

EXAMPLE 2.3   Pärt, *Solfeggio*, seven-tone row.

Throughout *Solfeggio*, the row appears only in its prime form. After it is sung ten times in succession—that is, after the C major scale is ascended ten times—the piece simply ends.

In *Solfeggio*, Pärt's fascination for rational design is paired with a radical restricting of the pitch materials made available for implementing that design, in a manner that anticipates the algorithmic processes he would employ in *Tabula Rasa* and some other early *tintinnabuli* works. In fact, the process of *Solfeggio*'s unfolding is so simple and transparent, and so completely determinative of the pitch content of the whole, that the piece might be heard in curious relation to such emblematic works of American experimentalism as Steve Reich's *Piano Phase* (1965) and *Four Organs* (1970), though neither Pärt nor Reich was aware of the other's efforts at the time. Much as Reich described his own music, so too does *Solfeggio* exemplify "pieces of music that are, literally, processes"—processes that listeners can plainly hear unfolding in real time.[13] At the turn of the century, in an interview with Hillier, Reich voiced his wonder at having recently encountered *Solfeggio* for the first time. "When you showed me the 1964 piece *Solfeggio*," Reich averred, "I thought that it was an enormously striking and interesting thing to see that Pärt basically had the gist of the whole thing in '64—to have a completely serialized, tightly organized C Major scale."[14]

As it happened, it was not *Solfeggio* but *Perpetuum Mobile* that gave Pärt his first taste of international success. A popular hit with audiences in Estonia from the time of its 1963 premiere, it was soon performed throughout the eastern bloc, in Venice and Paris, and in the United States.[15] Exemplifying a highly accessible approach to avant-garde composition, the work made Pärt into something of an idol for a still younger generation of composers emerging in Tallinn and Moscow. As one of Pärt's Estonian contemporaries recalled in an interview of the 1990s, the piece became a point of pride for some his compatriots, residents of a Soviet republic who had been subjected for a generation to official pronouncements about their cultural dependency upon Russian models. As the composer Eino Tamberg remarked, "Perhaps the public felt that it was something new, something newer than in Moscow, which was good for our nation. Perhaps we were kind of proud of it, of what we could create."[16]

Crucially, *Perpetuum Mobile* was warmly received in some corners of the official Soviet press as well. As a pair of musicologists wrote on the pages of *Sovetskaia muzyka* in 1966, "It might seem to be an elementary, formal study! But in fact *Perpetuum* makes a great impression on listeners. At first you perceive only some noisy process. But as it unfolds, there springs forth a multitude of associations."[17] These writers' observations about the work's tendency to call forth "associations" (*assotsiatsii*) in the mind of the listener might help to explain the surprising degree of acceptance that greeted it in official circles despite its dodecaphonic construction. Their words might also help us to account for the broader embrace of Pärt and his music by Soviet officialdom as the decade wore on. For as Schmelz observes of *Perpetuum Mobile* and some other works of the 1960s, Pärt's music effectively wedded serial procedures to "a sense of dramaturgy that accommodated Socialist Realist musical demands."[18] Those demands, which Pärt had learned to satisfy in *Our Garden* and *Stride of the World*, consisted in accessibility, evocativeness (an aptness to conjure "associations" with extramusical ideas or images), and a sense of drama that might be heard in relation to a potentially animating narrative. Beginning with Pärt's next large-scale work, his dodecaphonic First Symphony, nearly all of his compositions would be purchased by the Ministry of Culture.[19] His music, while still controversial at times and in some circles, was gradually becoming official.

Yet another aspect of Pärt's work of the 1960s bears consideration here, for it too anticipates the sounds and structures of *Tabula Rasa* directly. In his *Collage über B–A–C–H*, Pärt produced a novel and subsequently influential kind of stylistic mashup. The piece opens with a B♭ major triad played throughout the orchestra, which quickly yields to a gradual unfolding of a ten-note chromatic row, similar to what we have seen and heard in *Perpetuum Mobile* and *Solfeggio*. In *Collage*, the row begins with what is often called the musical "cipher" of Johann Sebastian Bach: the pitches B, A, C, and H in German nomenclature, or B♭, A, C, and B♮ in their English spellings (example 2.4).

EXAMPLE 2.4   Pärt, *Collage über B-A-C-H*, ten-tone row. The bracket shows the B-A-C-H motive.

The second movement of Pärt's work is a Baroque dance called a sarabande, which he constructed by setting phrases from the Sarabande movement of Bach's Sixth English Suite in alternation with dissonant tone clusters comprising all twelve pitches of the chromatic scale (▶ audio 2.6). *Collage* was the first of several collagelike works that Pärt would compose in the coming years. Once again, with this approach, he found a way of employing avant-garde techniques in an immediately accessible manner, infused with the potential for high drama that its jarring shifts and juxtapositions of disparate historical styles afforded.

In the early 1970s Alfred Schnittke would come to be recognized as the consummate master of such style-shifting music as this, which he described and theorized as "polystylism" (in Russian, *polistilistika*), and which he first encountered in *Collage* and other works by Pärt.[20] For Schnittke, polystylism comprised not only literal quotations like those in Pärt's second movement, but also more general allusions and means of importing "elements of another's style" into one's own compositions. It consists, he wrote, in invoking the "scents and shadows of other times in music."[21] And, much as other aspects of Pärt's work had already demonstrated for many, polystylism provided means, at least in theory, for yoking avant-garde idioms to the socialist realist project—for depicting aspects of Soviet reality, or possible realities, with an accessible, evocative, even dramatic musical language. "In spite of all the complications and possible dangers of polystylism," Schnittke suggested in an essay from around 1971,

> its merits are now obvious: a broadening of the range of expressive means and the expansion of possibilities for integrating

"low" and "high" styles, the "banal" and the "refined"; a broader musical world and a general democratization of style; documentary objectivity of musical reality, presented not merely as something reflected individually but through citation . . . [and] new possibilities for the musical, dramaturgical embodiment of "eternal" questions—of war and peace, of life and death.[22]

Accessible or not, what many consider Schnittke's first masterpiece of polystylistic composition, his First Symphony of 1971, was so unsparingly dark that it was impossible to reconcile with any niche of official music in the USSR. Premiered only three years later in the closed city of Gorky (now Nizhny Novgorod), it was played only once more prior to the advent of glasnost and perestroika: in Tallinn in early 1976, testifying once again to the relatively liberal climate of the Estonian capital.[23] But Schnittke stuck with polystylism for the long run, soon tempering his darkness with ironic humor and thus finding his own path into the official Soviet musical establishment. His polystylistic First Concerto Grosso (1977) was a critical success at home and abroad. As it happened, Schnittke's concerto was the very work for which *Tabula Rasa*—itself a polystylistic concerto—was conceived as a companion.

By the second half of the 1960s, Pärt had emerged as one of the most widely recognized Soviet composers of his generation. Some in Estonia feted him as a national treasure. In a book compiled in 1966 to promote the republic's music to a Western audience, images of Pärt literally framed the whole. Its opening pages featured a portrait of Pärt alongside Heino Eller, his teacher at the Conservatory, and Boris Kõrver, chairman of the Estonian branch of the Composers' Union

FIGURE 2.1 Pärt (*right*), with Boris Kõrver and Heino Eller, in Leo Normet and Artur Vahter, *Soviet Estonian Music* (Tallinn, 1967), 8.

(figure 2.1).[24] On its back cover was a photo of Pärt alone. Pärt's music was performed throughout the USSR and at prominent festivals in the "near abroad": Prague Spring in 1964, Warsaw Autumn in 1965, the Zagreb Biennale in 1967.[25] In 1968 *Sovetskaia muzyka* published a deeply appreciative analytical study of his First Symphony, complete with diagrams of its twelve-tone rows.[26] Another laudatory *Sovetskaia muzyka* article hailed the composer as an "ironic inventor, an audacious iconoclast, maybe even an 'Estonian Stravinsky.'"[27] But significantly, while the audacious side of Pärt's music and demeanor endeared him to audiences and critics alike, it was precisely that aspect of his personality that would bring this celebrated period of his career to a close. For in addition to his seemingly insatiable hunger for new modes of musical expression, Pärt indeed exhibited, in these early years, aspects of behavior consistent with the iconoclast. Just as his serial and collage-based works were beginning to be accepted by many, he began to engage in more daring projects that could not fail to alienate him from the authorities.

In the autumn of 1966 Pärt received a commission envisioned to commemorate the fiftieth anniversary of the October Revolution of 1917. As Schmelz documents, correspondence between Pärt and the Composers' Union in Moscow indicates that he fulfilled the commission with a composition (now lost) entitled "Op. 17"—the title apparently a joking reference to the revolutionary year. As a letter from a Union official made clear shortly after Op. 17 was received, the piece itself was a joke of sorts: a scandalously provocative play on the "Internationale," the USSR's national anthem, "fragments" of which, interspersed with "sonoristic episodes, effectively noise," Pärt arranged graphically on the page "in the form of a five-pointed star." The effect of the whole, explained the official, "seems to us more than dubious."[28]

In the end, Op. 17 did not offend beyond the confines of the Composers' Union, if only because it was suppressed as soon as it was received. But another project a few years later was more publicly provocative. In January 1968 Pärt participated in a work of performance art at the House of Writers in Tallinn, in which he and friends staged an "experimental evening" (*eksperimentaalõhtu*) involving a surgical mask, forceps, a white mouse, and a cheap violin. Perhaps by accident, their violin was burned by a candle or sparkler in the performance, in an unknowing echo of a notorious Fluxus performance by La Monte Young in New York.[29] The effect of the performance in Tallinn was deeply alienating for some who witnessed it or even heard about it. "It was not pretty," recalled the composer Jaan Rääts in an interview from the 1990s. A report by the Central Committee of the Estonian Communist Party called a performance a "nihilistic violin-burning." As one of Pärt's collaborators in the performance remembered the conversations that followed, "There was an Estonian writer, Johannes Semper, he was the only [one] who said, that this was good. The only one."[30]

The act that went furthest in terms of alienating Pärt from the authorities was the premiere of his *Credo* in November 1968, a composition for full orchestra, large choir, and piano. Another polystylistic or collage-based work, *Credo* consists in arresting juxtapositions of quotations from Bach—this time the C major Prelude from Book I of *The Well-Tempered Clavier*—with music newly composed in a Baroque manner (what Schnittke would call "quotation not of musical fragments but of the technique of another's style"), alongside aleatory and dodecaphonic passages.[31] As if to reveal the atonal potential lurking within the tonal system itself, the twelve-tone row Pärt used in *Credo* was nothing but the circle of fifths, the theoretical foundation of modulation in Western tonal music (example 2.5).

EXAMPLE 2.5   Pärt, *Credo*, twelve-tone row.

In performance *Credo* embodies a kind of drama that has endeared it to audiences to this day, with Bach and tonality seeming to stand for a vision of human good and divine purity, and with atonality apparently representing something approaching their opposites.[32] But what made the work so untenable within the officially atheistic Soviet Union was its text, which Pärt crafted by fusing his own adaptation of the Nicene Creed (*Credo in Jesum Christum:* "I believe in Jesus Christ") to Christ's Sermon on the Mount as recalled in the Gospel of Matthew ("You have heard that it was said, 'An eye for an eye and a tooth for a tooth'"). As Siitan writes of the work's premiere, Pärt's *Credo* was remarkable for the fact that "in the Soviet Union of that period, such an unambiguous proclamation of that way of thinking signaled a deliberate parting with official ideology."[33] It would have been risky to hazard such a proclamation of Christian faith—such an open rejection of Soviet values—in a private gathering. But *Credo* requires a hundred or more individuals to perform. Its premiere was led by Neeme Järvi, the most prominent conductor in the republic, and furthermore, it was broadcast live on Estonian radio.[34] Even in the relatively liberal environment of Tallinn, how did such an event ever take place?

The short answer is that we do not know, at least not with any certainty. In Kautny's archival digging and interviews with several of Pärt's Estonian contemporaries, no clear answers emerge. There is no mention of the work in minutes of meetings by the Estonian Composers' Union prior to the premiere, and it was not announced in published previews of Tallinn's 1968–69 concert season. Some suggest that Pärt's chances of having the work premiered were increased by its falling amidst a series of ambitious programs of Estonian music scheduled for performance in Moscow, East Germany, and Uzbekistan, which might have distracted key members of the Ministry of Culture from giving *Credo* the pre-performance vetting it would normally receive.[35] But still, how could it be that not one of the people involved in the rehearsals leaked word of its transparently religious nature? For lack of a fuller documentary record, we might turn to Pärt's own recollection of the event from an interview of 2003:

> As fate would have it, the most merciless member of the commission [the committee of the Composers' Union charged with previewing new works before their public premieres], who was also an eager servant of the Party and my archenemy, became ill on this very day [when *Credo* was to be considered]. I explained to those [committee members] who heard my *Credo* that I had used material taken from the first prelude of Bach's *Well-Tempered Clavier*. They felt good about this and thought the text was completely harmless, presumably because it was in Latin. In the end, the piece was accepted and performed.[36]

Any ignorance of the work's Christian subject was dispelled upon its premiere, however. Almost as soon as *Credo* was played, the hammer of officialdom came down. "I understood that the situation was serious and investigations were already under way at the highest level," Pärt recalled of the days that followed. "I was questioned several times, and the interrogators kept repeating the same question: 'What political aim are you pursuing with this work?'"[37]

As Siitan suggests, Pärt's open proclamation of Christian faith signaled a deliberate parting with official realms of music making and cultural activity in the Soviet Union. And Pärt was unapologetic, reaffirming his faith shortly after the premiere in an interview recorded for Estonian Radio, which was unsurprisingly censored before it aired (▶ video 2.1).[38] Nevertheless, Pärt did not become a persona non grata in Estonia or elsewhere in Soviet society. His new music—*Credo* excepted, of course—continued to be purchased by the Ministry of Culture. He was not expelled from the Composers' Union, and his compositions were still widely performed. Even *Credo* would be played again: in Soviet Georgia, a decade after its premiere.[39] After the 1968 event, no public denunciation occurred. In fact, as the Estonian journalist Immo Mihkelson notes, "the aftermath" of the premiere "was suppressed and kept hidden from the public sphere."[40] Pärt remembers "receiv[ing] orders never again to have this *Credo* performed, and never to show its score."[41] But as Savenko recalls, the fact that it was "practically"—though not, it seems, officially—"banned from performance" actually had the unintended effect of increasing the Soviet public's interest in Pärt and his music.[42] As Pärt's wife, Nora, recalled of the weeks that followed the premiere: "At the end of the year there was a sort of opinion poll in the local press. People were asked to name the most impressive cultural event in which they had taken part. Ninety percent of those questioned named this concert" at which *Credo* was played.[43]

By some measures, Pärt's productivity declined in the years after the *Credo* scandal, and in some respects he seemed to withdraw from the public stage. Compared to the middle years of the 1960s, he completed few new concert works. But this was not the "silent" period that some writers on the composer have described. In the half decade following the premiere of *Credo*, Pärt completed two works of concert music, both of which were substantially longer than any he had previously composed: his Third Symphony of 1971 and the seven movement, oratorio-like composition *Song to the Beloved* (*Laul armastatule*) of 1973.[44] In 1968 his resigned from his job as an engineer for Estonian Radio, which he had held for a decade, and he embarked on an intensive period of composing for Estonian film and television programs, which brought his music into the homes of countless individuals in Tallinn and beyond.[45] During these years other changes transpired in his creative and personal life. He discovered Gregorian chant and other medieval repertoires, the study of which he pursued with increasing fascination in the early 1970s. He met Nora and converted, as she had, to Orthodox Christianity in 1972.[46] And he continued to experiment with new means of construction and ordering in his work. At some point between the winter of 1975 and the autumn of 1976, a new round of experimentation would yield a style of writing that Pärt would christen *tintinnabuli*, a style upon which he would settle after nearly two decades of constant exploration, a style both new and of a piece with where he had been before.

CHAPTER 3
TINTINNABULI

Few stories about music in the late twentieth century are told with such fascination as Pärt's discovery of *tintinnabuli*, a style of music—or technique of writing music, or way of thinking about music—that he introduced to the world in 1976, and in which he has composed nearly all of his subsequent work. From shortly after his emigration from the USSR in 1980, much has been written on the formal designs of Pärt's *tintinnabuli* constructions.[1] Far less has been said about how *tintinnabuli* might inflect the experience of music more broadly, or about what we might call its ontologies: what *tintinnabuli* can be said to *be*. From the start, Pärt's use of the term was unstable and freighted with metaphorical, even metaphysical commentary, and the sounds of *tintinnabuli* have always been treated in popular discourse as somewhat ineffable. The first task of this chapter will be to outline what most listeners would seem to agree on: how *tintinnabuli*, as a structure or technique, is manifested in Pärt's music. Then I will turn to history, sketching Pärt's discovery of *tintinnabuli* and asking what the term has connoted in relation to the evolution of his work and career. Finally, I will ask what else the word might signify or imply, beyond or above the notes inscribed on the pages of Pärt's scores.

SOUNDS

In his pioneering study of Pärt's life and works, Paul Hillier proposed a theoretical language for describing the basics of the composer's *tintinnabuli* constructions. Later elaborated and refined by others, Hillier's terminology has become a kind of lingua franca in discussions of Pärt's music.[2] As Hillier presents it, *tintinnabuli* can be said to consist essentially in two voices or lines: a melodic voice or "M-voice," and a *tintinnabuli* voice or "T-voice." The M-voice may follow any course determined by the composer, while the T-voice accompanies or shadows the M-voice by moving among pitches of a single triad in a manner determined according to some prearranged relationship between the two voices. To see how this works, consider an example from one of Pärt's earliest *tintinnabuli* compositions, the polystylistic *If Bach Had Kept Bees* (1976) (example 3.1, ▶ audio 3.1).

EXAMPLE 3.1 Pärt, *If Bach Had Kept Bees*, mm. 128–34.

At the start of this passage, Pärt borrows the M-voice, played pizzicato by cellos and basses, from the B minor Prelude from the first book of Bach's *Well-Tempered Clavier*. He doubles the durations of Bach's pitches, so that Bach's eighth notes (in the keyboard's left hand) become quarter notes in Pärt's setting (example 3.2, ▶ audio 3.2).

EXAMPLE 3.2 J. S. Bach, B minor Prelude from *The Well-Tempered Clavier*, Book I, mm. 1–4.

(My discussion here refers to the published version of Pärt's score, most recently revised in 2001; in the 1976 original, the M-voice was played by trombones.)[3]

In example 3.1, the T-voice enters in measure 129, played by violas. It consists solely of pitches of the B minor triad (B, D, and F♯), articulated according to a prearranged rule. In this case, the rule specifies that the T-voice sounds the closest pitch of the B minor triad above or below the M-voice pitch with which it is paired, alternating between triadic pitches immediately below and just above the notes of the M-voice. In measure 129, the first pitch in the M-voice (in cellos and basses) is F♯. The closest member of the B minor triad below that F♯ is D, so the first pitch in the T-voice, played by violas, is a D. The second pitch in the M-voice, also in measure 129, is G♯; the closest member of the B minor triad *above* that G♯ is B, so the second pitch of the T-voice, again played by violas, is B. Throughout example 3.1, this relationship is maintained, with cellos and basses playing the M-voice in quarter notes, and with violas playing a T-voice that consists of the nearest pitch of the B minor triad, alternating between triadic pitches below and above each note of the M-voice.

In measure 130, a second M-voice enters, played by the second violins in half notes. It is taken from an accompanying line—the top line—of Bach's prelude, again doubling the durations of Bach's pitches (compare the second violin's line in example 3.1, m. 130, with the top line in example 3.2, m. 2). In measure 131, Pärt has the first violins play a T-voice to the second violins' M-voice according to the same rule as that used before, only this time reversing the order of oscillations above and below the M-voice. In measure 131 of example 3.1, the first violins' T-voice consists of an F♯, the closest member of the B minor triad *above* the D in the second violins' M-voice. On the third beat of measure 132, the first violins' T-voice sounds a B, the closest member of the B minor triad *below* the second violins' M-voice C♯. All of Pärt's *tintinnabuli* works feature some version of these structures, with one or more M-voices shadowed by one or more T-voices, and with the pitches of the latter bearing some consistent, predetermined relationship to the notes of the M-voice.

One of the hallmarks of *tintinnabuli* is its play with what the Russian music theorist Elena Tokun calls *tonal'nye priznaki*: tonal signs or intimations.[4] These intimations are owed to the fact that the T-voice consists simply in movement between and among the three constituent pitches of a major or (more often) minor triad, perhaps the most fundamental building block of musical construction in the Western tonal system. In *If Bach Had Kept Bees*, Pärt took his M-voice from a preexisting tonal work, which reinforces all the more strongly the listener's sense of tonal intimation. In all of Pärt's *tintinnabuli* music, regardless of whether the M-voice is borrowed from elsewhere or newly composed, the sounding of the M-voice against a stable triad in the T-voice creates an audible sense of frequent, even cyclical dissolution of consonance into dissonance and then back into consonance, similar to the ebb and flow of consonance and dissonance characteristic of tonal music.

And yet, the juxtaposition of T- and M-voices does not yield a tonal composition. First, the retention of a single triad in the T-voice over an extensive span of time, or even for the entire length of a work, does not provide for modulation or the polarity of tonic and dominant key areas that is a defining feature of Western tonality. Moreover, the simultaneous sounding of M- and T-voices—even when both of those voices share an ostensible key, as in the B minor world of *If Bach Had Kept Bees*—yields dissonances that are neither prepared nor resolved according to normative rules of tonal counterpoint. In example 3.1, dissonances are abundant and acute in measures 131–33, where jarring major and minor seconds sound between the cellos' M-voice and the violas' T-voice on successive beats of every bar: beats 2 and 3 in measure 131, beats 1 and 2 in measure 132, and beats 3 and 4 in measure 133. It is as if the triad is revealed in *tintinnabuli* to harbor the potential to give rise to radical, even jarring dissonance, a "profound world of dissonance"—to quote the musicologist Maria Cizmic—"that arises when these [tonal] materials freely interact with one another."[5] It is a revelation akin to what Pärt had earlier attempted in *Solfeggio*, with its serial treatment of an ascending C major scale, and in *Credo*, with its twelve-note row assembled by traversing the circle of fifths. But in contrast to those earlier works, *tintinnabuli*, with its grounding in an immovable triad, promises the listener an eventual, even inevitable resolution—or dissolution, or at least *potential* for dissolution—of the audible tension its dissonance creates.

In conversation, Pärt has often remarked on the tonal intimations that pervade the nontonal sounds of *tintinnabuli*. "As the foundation of the T-voice," he once explained, "the triad is freed from its traditional context," divorced from its customarily functional role. Instead, the triad appears like "an independent force, a kind of 'solid plateau'" upon which the M-voice sounds.[6] Or, as he explained on another occasion, invoking a favorite numerical metaphor for the relation of M- and T-voices, the sounding together of those two lines "does not comprise harmony in a conventional sense, and it is perhaps not true polyphony either. It is something completely different. It is as if one were to say that $1 + 1 = 1$."[7] With this, Pärt seems to suggest that although *tintinnabuli* consists in the simultaneous sounding of two distinct lines (M- and T-voices), their superposition does not constitute a tonal structure, or even a polyphonic setting that abides by traditional rules of tonal or modal counterpoint. Rather, the two lines reflect each other's movements according to a prearranged schema. They are two sounding manifestations of a single musical idea, the one embodying stepwise motion and the other reflecting that motion in triadic space. It is, perhaps, like an individual regarding her face in the mirror, or like a singer and his echo: they are distinct and different, yet one and the same.[8]

The term itself, *tintinnabuli*, is Latin for "little bells." Some of the earliest performances of Pärt's works to consist in juxtaposition of M- and T-voices were accompanied by notes the composer prepared in collaboration with his wife, Nora, where they described the bell-like sounds that his latest music might convey. In an explanatory essay written for distribution at the first official public concert of Pärt's *tintinnabuli* music on October 27, 1976, and subsequently reprinted for performances in Leningrad and Tallinn in 1977–78, Nora explained:

> A natural sense of euphony or balance, harmony and purity, is confirmed by the general heading, "Little Bells" (*Tintinnabuli*). The beauty of the natural sound of the little bell [*kolokol'chika*] is associated by the author [i.e., Pärt] with the idea of euphony and, more specifically, with the triad. It is as if the composer were playing with these ideas, connecting them with each other at will and bringing them together. In the author's words, "the triad provided the basis for *Tintinnabuli*, not only with respect to intonation, but also in terms of construction and form."[9]

While laying out an explanation for what listeners were likely to hear as a new direction in Pärt's work, this statement also signals that the advent of *tintinnabuli* did not necessarily mark a wholesale departure from his earlier concerns. For by invoking the term *intonation* (in the Pärts' Russian, *intonatsionnaia osnova*, or "intonational basis"), the essay seems to point, at least obliquely, to the tradition of socialist realism that had inflected the reception of the composer's avant-garde experiments since the early 1960s. "Intonation" (*intonatsiia*) was a theoretical term coined by the Soviet musicologist Boris Asaf'ev in the 1940s to describe a musical quotation or allusion to sounds or ideas in the natural or social world. It was a tool with which composers were expected to create music that reflected Soviet reality in a celebratory or idealizing way.[10] In the manner of such an intonation, the harmony and euphony, purity and balance that the Pärts asked their audiences to hear in *tintinnabuli* were offered as echoes, glimpses, or reflections of a surrounding, imaginary world. Perhaps it was the world of Tallinn's Old Town, studded with the domes, spires, and bells of centuries-old Lutheran and Orthodox churches. Or perhaps the Pärts invoked Asaf'ev's language in service of a more provocative project, one that harbored the potential to disrupt the very worldview that socialist realism was intended to uphold. Perhaps the world they glimpsed was an inner space, one of quiet, meditation, even prayer.

DISCOVERIES

As he relayed in an interview of 2000 with the viola da gamba player Jordi Savall, Pärt's discovery of *tintinnabuli* came after a period of creative crisis and introspection during which the only constants in his musical world were Gregorian chant and other medieval musics he had recently encountered. Echoing Gustav Mahler, who famously described his own creative crisis of 1907–8 as compelling him "to learn to stand and walk all over again like a beginner,"[11] Pärt recounted his period of searching as follows:

> In the beginning, during my twelve-tone period, I lived truly separated from original sources. And the turn I took, it was a matter of learning how to walk all over again. Undoubtedly, the reason such a metamorphosis takes place in certain people and not in others will forever remain a riddle; all I know is that when I heard Gregorian chant for the first time, I must have been mature enough, in one way or another, to be able to appreciate such musical richness. At that moment I felt at once utterly deprived and rich. Utterly naked, too. I felt like the prodigal son returning to his father's home. I had nothing, I had accomplished nothing. The methods I had used before had not allowed me to say what I wanted to say with music,

yet I did not know any others. At that moment, my previous work seemed like an attempt to carry water with a sieve. I was absolutely certain: everything I had done until then I would never do again .... I had to start again from scratch. It took me seven, eight years before I felt the least bit of confidence—a period during which I listened to and studied a lot of early music.[12]

The roots of Pärt's crisis of the late 1960s and early '70s are undoubtedly complex and ultimately unknowable. They manifested in a prolonged period of spiritual transition, during which time he converted to Orthodoxy, and an even longer period of creative uncertainty.[13] Speaking of the crossroads at which the composer found himself after the premiere of *Credo* in 1968, Toomas Siitan suggests that Pärt became painfully aware of what seemed an irreconcilable conflict between his abiding desire to create broadly accessible music, as he had done in *Our Garden* and his film scores, and his commitment to the rational structures and mathematical logic of serial composition. For Siitan, this conflict was vividly embodied in the tormented sounds of *Credo* itself, a work in which "the dualism regarding the content and style of earlier compositions reached an agonizing simplicity with no way forward."[14]

We do not know exactly when Pärt encountered Gregorian chant for the first time. But the most striking testament to his period of searching might be a collection of over three hundred notebooks preserved at the Arvo Pärt Centre in Laulasmaa, Estonia, which record his attempts to teach himself to compose melodies in a manner akin to Gregorian chant, sometimes setting texts from the Psalms or taking graphic inspiration from features of the natural landscape (▶ video 3.1).¹⁵ It was in these notebooks, which Pärt began filling (or at least dating and saving) in 1975, that the musicologist Saale Kareda found the earliest notated incidence of *tintinnabuli* in the form of a nearly complete sketch of *Für Alina*, dated February 7, 1975—though the Pärts have recently affirmed that the year of composition was actually 1976 (▶ video 3.2).¹⁶ That work was among those unveiled in the first official public concert of Pärt's *tintinnabuli* music. But the chronology is complicated, for Pärt's use of chantlike melodies in his work began before he started filling his notebooks, as evinced in his Third Symphony of 1971 and *Song to the Beloved* of 1973 (▶ audio 3.3).¹⁷ Moreover, many of his early *tintinnabuli* works— including *In Spe* from the 1976 concert, and also *Tabula Rasa*—find their M-voices in another manner entirely, one more consistent with his serial experiments of the previous decade: in the strict unfolding of predetermined algorithms or processes.

Further testifying to Pärt's engagement with medieval music in these years were his collaborations with the violinist Andres Mustonen, whose early music ensemble Hortus Musicus, founded in Tallinn in 1972, became a kind of "creative workshop" for the composer as his first *tintinnabuli* works were taking shape. Pärt recalls bringing sketches of his experiments to the Hortus musicians, who would play them on such medieval and Renaissance instruments as the viola da gamba, recorder, and crumhorn.¹⁸ It was Hortus Musicus that gave the signal concert of Pärt's *tintinnabuli* music in October 1976, in a program that paired Pärt's works with a mass by the fifteenth-century composer Guillaume Dufay (figure 3.1). Hortus also played parts of *Tabula Rasa*

ПРОГРАММА

I

А. ПЯРТ — Tintinnabuli
(1935) (первое исполнение)
  Galix
  Modus
  Trivium
  К Алине
  Если бы Бах разводил пчел...
  Pari intervallo
  In spe

Участвует —
заслуженный коллектив ЭССР
Таллинский камерный хор

Хормейстеры —
народный артист ЭССР
Куно Аренг

заслуженный деятель искусств ЭССР
Антс Юлеоя

Партия органа —
РОЛЬФ УУСВЯЛИ

FIGURE 3.1 Program for the first official public performance (*pervoe ispolnenie*) of Pärt's *tintinnabuli* music, October 27, 1976, with Hortus Musicus, directed by Andres Mustonen, at the Estonia Concert Hall in Tallinn. The seven works by Pärt include *Calix* (here *Galix*), later reworked as the *Dies Irae* section of *Miserere* (1989); *Modus*, a revision of which would be published as *Sarah*

II

Г. ДЮФАИ — Месса
(1400—1474) «L'homme arme»
1. Kyrie
2. Gloria
3. Credo
4. Sanctus
5. Agnus Dei

Состав ансамбля:

Хелле Мустонен (сопрано)

Марье Тралла (альт)

Йозеп Вахермяги (тенор)

Рихо Ридбек (бас)

Андрес Мустонен (pardessus de viola, блокфлёте, ударные, крумхорн)

Тайво Нийтвяги (блокфлёте, ударные, крумхорн)

Тынис Куурме (блокфлёте, крумхорн, фагот)

Хенн Ребане (шалмей, гитара)

Райво Тарум (цинк, труба)

Вальтер Юргенсон (тромбон)

Пэетер Клаас (виола да гамба)

Тыну Рейн (клавесин)

Художественный руководитель ансамбля —
АНДРЕС МУСТОНЕН

Was Ninety Years Old (1989); *K Aline* (*Für Alina*); *Esli by Bakh razvodil pchel* (*If Bach Had Kept Bees*); and *In Spe*, which Pärt would publish in 1984 as *An den Wassern zu Babel saßen wir und weinten*. The second half of the concert featured Dufay's *L'homme armé* Mass. Estonian Theatre and Music Museum, M238/1:4. Used by permission.

for Pärt while it was taking shape.[19] An archival recording of the 1976 concert reveals a distinctly "early music" sound to the performance, if not a strictly medieval one. Later published for piano, *Für Alina* was played by viols accompanied by tinkling bells and a choir. *Pari Intervallo*, later published for organ, was performed with viols, recorders, and a xylophone. A harpsichord played parts of *Modus* that would be assigned to voices when it was later published as *Sarah Was Ninety Years Old*.[20]

Moreover, when Pärt emerged publicly from his period of uncertainty with the October concert, much of what he unveiled might well seem related to his earlier experiments. I have already pointed to the Pärts' invocation of the language of socialist realism in the concert program, to the algorithmic processes used to generate the pitch material of *In Spe* and other works, to ways in which the tonal intimations of *tintinnabuli* recall *Solfeggio* and *Credo*, and to Pärt's continued interest in polystylism, as evinced in *If Bach Had Kept Bees*. Beyond these things, a number of his statements reveal fundamental continuities in his thinking about his music that extend from the 1960s all the way into the 2000s. Reflecting in 2003 upon his early serial experiments, he invoked their sounding "portrait of an unearthly world, in which human suffering had been removed in order to make room for a more objective and distanced view of things." He continued: "At that time I was convinced that every mathematical formula could be translated into music. I thought that, in this way, one could create purer and more objective music. If I had been able to create a completely emotion free music, then I would have been able to distance myself from dodecaphonic music."[21] With his discovery of *tintinnabuli*, he clearly succeeded in distancing himself from the sounds of dodecaphony. But his aspiration to create an objective or "emotion free" music endured. In that same conversation from 2003, he described his *Arbos*, a *tintinnabuli* work from 1977, as "pure mathematics" (*reine Mathematik*), and elsewhere he called *Summa*, another work of that year, "one of my computer music pieces" (*eine von meinen Computermusiken*).[22] Ten years earlier he had told the critic John Rockwell: "I don't own a computer, but there is a computer in my mind and heart."[23] Earlier still, in the program notes for the *tintinnabuli* concert of October 1976, Nora Pärt observed: "Never before has number or mathematical calculation appeared in the work of a composer in such a naked way, as if to emphasize the beauty of its true essence."[24] The following year, in notes distributed at the premiere of *Tabula Rasa*, the Pärts urged attendees to listen with ears attuned to the "strictness of the mathematical structure."[25]

It is here, perhaps, that Pärt's relation to the Western postwar modernist legacy of Schoenberg, Boulez, Cage, and others is most vividly revealed. For, as Richard Taruskin has argued, what all those artists had in common was a search for ways of creating music "that put one in touch with something less vulnerable than personal wishes and tastes, or subjective standards of beauty."[26] As Taruskin understands it, their common aspirations were forged in response to the anxieties—even existential terrors—of the postwar, Cold War world. For "after Hiroshima," Taruskin writes (or after Auschwitz, Stalinism, or the publication of Solzhenitsyn's work, in *samizdat* and in the West), "everyone felt like dirt. The only responsible decision left was to face that miserable contingency and find a way of composing that would stamp out the artist's puny person and allow something 'realer' to emerge." For many, this "desperate antihumanism," as Taruskin calls it, "sought its consolation in an ancient prehumanism." For Cage, the latter consisted in Zen; for Boulez, in a kind of romantic medievalism. In both of their cases, consolation "rested on a Platonic (and before Plato, a Pythagorean) faith in number as the ultimate and imperishable reality." For "what," Taruskin asks, "could be realer"—or more permanent, or more wholly transcendent of human frailty and suffering—"than number?" As Pärt stressed to Savall and others, his early dodecaphonic work was, at least in hindsight, a music of existential despair. In this light, his enduring Neoplatonic fascination with number was something he shared with many.

Nevertheless, sometime between the late 1960s and the early '80s—with his conversion to Orthodoxy and his marriage, with his emigration to the West and the general passing of time—Pärt's dispiriting if widely shared views gave way to something else: to an almost laserlike focus on consolation, to a search for something lasting and meaningful above and beyond the histories and trials of turbulent and traumatic human existence. For just as Pärt was discovering *tintinnabuli*, so he was also—through the vehicles of faith, family, and unceasing work—finding a habitable path, or at least a point of convalescence or repose, in the midst of the surrounding morass. Maybe more than his music, his outlook changed, yet his essentially Platonist vision remained. And that, I think, might well have been the greatest transformation of all in his creative life. What separated the composer of 1976 from the artist who had lived and worked before that year was not simply the discovery of *tintinnabuli*.

Rather, it was the fact that, once he found it, he clung to the technique as if to anchor his life of previously unmoored explorations. Throughout all his subsequent experiments with chantlike melodies, algorithmic designs, polystylism, and the rest, the sounds of *tintinnabuli* would ring in the background, grounding his work in a transcendent vision of something stable, lasting, and beautiful.

ONTOLOGIES

Pärt has often turned to metaphor when trying to describe the transcendent space or mode of being he hears or seeks in *tintinnabuli*. On the relationship between T- and M-voices, he once remarked: "as a child resembles his parents, so does the *tintinnabuli* voice carry the genes of the melody in itself." He immediately added: "perhaps I could also say that the melodic voice represents my sins and my imperfect nature, whereas the second [i.e., *tintinnabuli*] voice is the forgiveness granted to me. In this case, my subjective transgressions are corrected."[27] Of course, simple analogies must fail to hold, and it is easy to find moments in Pärt's music to confound them. For instance, if the M-voice is sin and the T-voice is forgiveness, then how do we explain those passages in *Passio* (1982) where Pontius Pilate, sitting in judgment of Christ, sings his words to a T-voice alone, as if reflecting an imaginary M-voice that is nowhere sounded in the score?[28] And how can we account for the moving conclusion of *If Bach Had Kept Bees*, where the T-voices fall silent six measures before the end, allowing the work to close with Bach's M-voices alone, and with a tonal cadence in the bright parallel key of B major?

It is possible that other, more fundamental aspects of Pärt's statements are metaphorical as well. For in the Soviet world in which *tintinnabuli* arose, his remarks about mathematics and early music could mean many things. Looking back from the vantage point of West Berlin in 1987, Pärt recalled his discovery of Gregorian chant somewhat differently than he later would to Savall. "I believe that this music was so attractive to me," he reflected, "not because of the music but rather because of religion. For me, religion was the principal problem, and in Gregorian chant I found what I was thirsting for."[29] For many artists of Pärt's generation living and working in the USSR, chant and other early musics offered a "back door to religious experience," as Taruskin describes it—a way to ponder and perform and even compose as an expression of one's faith, without hazarding the kind of explicit declaration for which Pärt was censured after the premiere of *Credo*.[30] But for many, the relation was perhaps better framed the other way around, with the study of early music being a natural outgrowth or even a byproduct of their religious searching. As the Russian pianist Alexei Liubimov recalled the relationship between his own musical activities to his spiritual explorations of the 1970s, in a statement that echoes Pärt's on chant, music "was a purely utilitarian pursuit, in some sense a creative one, but it was secondary at that time."[31]

The mathematical, even scientific bent to the Pärts' early statements on *tintinnabuli* might likewise have reflected spiritual experience, for such language could be used to couch one's religious concerns in ideologically neutral terms. As the musicologist Urve Lippus has written, a great deal of Estonian musicology in the 1970s was characterized by an outsized emphasis on objective, quantitative research methods. These served, she writes, to "associate one's work with the technological progress so highly prized by Soviet authorities," while at the same time enabling one's engagement with materials that would otherwise be unacceptable to the regime.[32] If Pärt's experiments with early music constituted a means of wrestling with his "principal problem," as he put it, then his accounts of their results in the language of mathematics might have allowed him to speak publicly about what he found.

And yet, the fact that Pärt has stuck with the language of mathematics for decades after leaving the USSR suggests that its significance for his journey cannot be attributed solely to his need to navigate life under a repressive regime. In fact, the Neoplatonic visions to which his statements on musical structure seem to point are reflected in his broader accounts of his discovery of *tintinnabuli* itself.[33] As the ethnomusicologist Philip V. Bohlman observes, what all Neoplatonic conceptions of music respond to is a fundamental question: about whether there is music "out there" in the world, "waiting to be discovered" by its eventual composer. Invariably, such visions answer in the affirmative, "mak[ing] claims for a mathematical and physical order that music ultimately articulates when it comes into existence."[34] On several occasions, Pärt has described his discovery of *tintinnabuli* literally as a discovery, his discovery of something that already existed somewhere, as if waiting to be articulated into awareness. As Kareda writes, relating a discussion she had with the composer in the 1990s, "Pärt says that at the root of every *tintinnabuli* work lies a 'formula' according to which the entire work is programmed in advance.... When I asked whether Pärt discovered or invented these formulas that were not previously described, he answered: 'I try to invent what already exists.'"[35] Or, as the composer remarked in an interview recorded for West German Radio, "What we discover in the world is already here. These laws are always valid. Suddenly we discover something and say: 'Ah, that is so!' But that was already so, it has always been so, before Einstein and before Newton, for thousands of years. It's the same in music. Music is here, music is there; and then someone comes along and hears it and writes it down. It is so."[36]

In Pärt's view, *tintinnabuli* was not his invention but his discovery of something already in the world, something ontologically prior to its first sounding by the players of Hortus Musicus, and prior also to its first inscription in Pärt's chant-filled notebooks. It might be that *If Bach Had Kept Bees* illustrates this vision more clearly than many of his works, for much of the piece, including all of its final thirty-six measures (beginning in example 3.1), consists solely in the addition of T-voices to music previously composed by Bach. Or perhaps one could suggest that the work consists not in Pärt's composition at all, but in his revealing of the reflections of Bach's melodic lines in the triadic space of *tintinnabuli*, made audible for the first time in the light of Pärt's musical mirror.[37] This possibility leads us to ask: If we hear the triadic voices in example 3.1 not as T-voices created by Pärt, but as voices that Pärt discovered when listening in a certain way to Bach's prelude, then might we also hear, if we listen in just the right way, similar T-voices sounding as reflections of every other musical utterance, whether or not those T-voices have yet been made audible by composers, voices, or instruments?

From the Neoplatonic perspective on *tintinnabuli* that Pärt seems to hold, the answer, I think, must be *yes*.

There might be still more to it than this, something that links Pärt's enduring fascination with number back to his "principal problem" in a way that transcends the postwar histories inscribed by the arc of his life. For as Jeffers Engelhardt has observed in his study of musical practice in the Orthodox Church of Estonia, aspects of that practice consist in attendance to a number of "Neoplatonic ontologies." As the icon painter in the Orthodox tradition renders visages of the saints in a manner thought to reflect their essence and permanence rather than their individuality, so too the Orthodox singer submits herself to the melodic "prototypes" of Orthodox modal systems rather than seeking to perform in an individuating, personally expressive way. It is through such singing—through such "disciplining, emptying, and effacing a desirous, individuated self" so that the spirit itself can be heard—that the Orthodox singer strives to know or become closer to God.[38] In Pärt's view, his task as a composer seems akin to this: to listen for the resonance of spirit and to shape his works as echoes of its sounds. This, I think, is what he seeks through the means of *tintinnabuli*. And with respect to this, it matters little whether we hear echoes of chant in his compositions, share in his experience of Orthodox spirituality, or follow his mathematical structures as we listen. For Pärt, the Holy Spirit pervades and animates the world. Like everything else within that world, his discovery of *tintinnabuli* would have been impossible if not for that transcendent ground.

In her program notes for the official unveiling of Pärt's *tintinnabuli* music, Nora Pärt downplayed the significance of the Latin title. "Seven independent compositions," she called the suite of works performed. "The general heading binds them only as the title of the opus."[39] An ambiguous clarification, to be sure. But in hindsight, as a statement from the Arvo Pärt Centre explains, "at that time, in 1976, neither Arvo nor Nora knew exactly what the term or concept might actually refer to: perhaps it was only to a group of musical works? Perhaps it was a new style? Or a compositional method or technique?"[40] One of the seven works on the concert—*Modus*—did not consist in the juxtaposition of M- and T-voices that has since become a hallmark of the *tintinnabuli* style. And as Hortus Musicus continued to perform Pärt's *Tintinnabuli* "opus" in the following years, its constituent works kept changing. In a performance given in Tallinn in May 1978, *Tintinnabuli* consisted of five compositions, none of which were included in the concert of 1976. The following December, Hortus brought *Tintinnabuli* to Leningrad, where ten compositions were included.[41]

Before the official unveiling of *Tintinnabuli*, the event was previewed and promoted on a *Soviet Estonia* newsreel.[42] Afterward it was reported that nearly a thousand people had tried to obtain tickets. Mustonen recalled the concert as having been completely sold out, but the Estonian journalist Immo Mihkelson estimates that the hall was "only at 80 percent capacity."[43] As Mustonen remembers,

> The reaction of the public was shock, because this was such simple music. Everywhere else music was very complicated. In Pärt's work too, there was always a lot of drama…. [Pärt's] Third Symphony was a transition, but otherwise all of his works

were very dramatic, like his Second Symphony. And then came this less dramatic music: only rhythms, only lines.... It was not yet clear if anything would come of this.[44]

For the composer as well, it was unclear whether anything would come of his *tintinnabuli* experiment. As he confided to the musicologist Enzo Restagno in 2003, recalling his first elaboration of *tintinnabuli* in his notebook sketch for *Für Alina*, "I had serious doubts about whether this thing I had created was really music.... This composition seemed too simple to me. My ears were not accustomed to taking such a work seriously.... I was tormented by thousands of such doubts."[45] Pärt qualified his remark by saying that his period of doubt did not last long. But later in the same interview, he and his wife provided a remarkable glimpse of just how long he was in fact tormented. As Nora recalled, the premiere of *Passio* in 1982 was "not a success," and "for many years Arvo was unsure about the quality of the composition."[46] She explained that it was not until after hearing the work recorded—six years later by Paul Hillier's Hilliard Ensemble—that her husband changed his mind. The composer then picked up Nora's account, referring to the example of *An den Wassern zu Babel*, which had premiered at the concert of 1976 under the title *In Spe*. Even with respect to that composition, one of his very first *tintinnabuli* works, "the same situation was repeated." It was not until he heard the Hilliard Ensemble's recording—made in 1986, ten years after the historic premiere—that he became convinced of the work's value. "Only then," he remembered, "did I become aware that I had made the right choice with my compositional technique, and I understood that this kind of music truly was viable."[47]

For others, the viability of *tintinnabuli* was confirmed more quickly, at a concert in September 1977 in the Great Hall of Tallinn's Technical University. The program featured Schnittke's First Concerto Grosso, composed for the violinists Kremer and Grindenko. But its highlight for many was the premiere of Pärt's newest *tintinnabuli* work, dedicated to the same pair of soloists: *Tabula Rasa*.[48] Soon, with Grindenko and Kremer, backed by the Lithuanian Chamber Orchestra and Schnittke himself at the prepared piano, *Tabula Rasa* would transcend the boundaries of Estonia and the Soviet Union itself, bringing Pärt and *tintinnabuli* to the attention of the world.

CHAPTER 4
TABULA RASA
LISTENING, READING

WORK ON *TABULA RASA* began shortly after the first official *tintinnabuli* concert of October 1976. The previous May, Kremer and Grindenko had asked Alfred Schnittke to provide them with a concerto grosso—a Baroque genre showcasing the skills of two or more soloists—to perform with the Lithuanian Chamber Orchestra and its conductor, Saulius Sondeckis. Schnittke obliged, and the following March they premiered the new work (now known as his Concerto Grosso No. 1) in Leningrad. Afterward the soloists made plans to take Schnittke's concerto on the road, on a tour that would run through the Soviet Union, West Germany, and Austria. In preparation for their upcoming visit to Tallinn in

September 1977, where they planned to perform Schnittke's piece with the Estonian conductor Eri Klas, Kremer and Grindenko invited Pärt to write something for the same ensemble Schnittke had used: a pair of violin soloists, string orchestra, and amplified prepared piano. "I limited myself to asking him whether he would be prepared to play very slow music," Pärt recalled of his initial conversation with Kremer, "and he answered that he had no problem with that."[1]

Despite Pärt's words to Kremer about the work he intended to write, what he delivered in the summer of 1977 was wholly unexpected.[2] In later years, both Kremer and Grindenko reflected on their first impressions of Pärt's score. Both are worth quoting at length for their accounts of a piece totally unlike anything they had seen before, which demanded modes of attention and performance that its players had to invent on the fly. "When Arvo was still thinking about *Tabula Rasa*," Kremer recounted in 1997, "he asked me whether he might compose something simple, something quiet."

> "Of course," I replied, trusting that he would be kind to me. What ultimately arrived looked remarkably simple, even provocatively so. Yet it was also exceptionally delicate. It was not just the fact that page after page was filled with a single harmony, mostly A minor, which required enormous precision from everyone with respect to intonation—from the soloists, Tatiana Grindenko and myself, and from the orchestra led by Eri Klas. It also demanded concentration, which was not apparent to us right away, but which hit us like a ton of bricks after we'd experienced playing all the long notes. Nothing can be allowed to destroy the condition of absolute stillness (*senza moto*) in the

second movement. For seventeen minutes [the duration of the movement] one hardly dared to breathe, because there was the danger it would affect the movement of the bow.³

In an interview of 2003 with the Russian musicologist Elena Dvoskina, Grindenko recalled the score of *Tabula Rasa* as surprising for the orchestra's players as well (figure 4.1). Its harmonic stasis suggested nothing of the drama heard in most symphonic music, and its score featured none of the expressive markings that musicians typically use to guide their playing. So, confronted with what they regarded as a piece that called out for their own interpretations, the musicians set about trying to supply the expressive gestures they believed were needed. After recalling an initial meeting with Pärt in the Latvian capital, Grindenko described the musicians' efforts:

> [Grindenko:] After that [i.e., after Pärt's discovery of *tintinnabuli*], we met entirely by chance at a festival in Riga, where I was taking part in some avant-garde concerts. I made his acquaintance and invited him to write something, with the guarantee that Gidon and I would perform it. When he had nearly finished, all the performers were really troubled by the second movement. At that time, people in classical circles had no precedent for such a musical meditation. This was, perhaps, the first such case. I remember how, in rehearsal, the musicians of the orchestra with which we were playing kept trying to make something out of the score, to intensify a bit, to pull back a bit . . .
>
> [Dvoskina:] A "dramatic unfolding" . . .
>
> [Grindenko:] Yes, like you might do with Brahms. It was impossible to get them to simply play it as it is, without adding anything more. Then, just before the beginning, Arvo came out on

stage, put his hands together as if in prayer, and said: "I implore you, there's no need to rescue my music." That moment has stayed with me in memory.[4]

Perhaps the most dramatic account of preparations for the premiere comes from the composer's wife, Nora (figures 4.1 and 4.2 show scenes from the rehearsals):

> So Arvo composed the piece, and Gidon Kremer and Tatiana Grindenko got *Tabula Rasa*. At the first rehearsal, they didn't have the slightest idea how the work could be played. But things got even worse when rehearsals with the orchestra began. Gidon must have thought he'd landed himself a huge problem when he'd asked for the piece. The conductor, Eri Klas, went to great lengths, and Schnittke [who was playing the prepared piano]

FIGURE 4.1   *Left to right*: Gidon Kremer, Tatiana Grindenko, and Eri Klas in rehearsal for the premiere of *Tabula Rasa* in September 1977. Note the unusual arrangement of the orchestral musicians. Estonian Theatre and Music Museum, M238:1/27. Used by permission.

FIGURE 4.2   Pärt during rehearsals for the premiere of *Tabula Rasa* in 1977. Estonian Theatre and Music Museum, M238:1/11; and Arvo Pärt Centre. Used by permission.

tried to save whatever he could. He went so far as to suggest that the orchestra's players be rearranged onstage, but it didn't make any difference. After two or three more rehearsals, the musicians put their instruments back in their cases and told us, "We can do no more." A few hours later we all arrived at the concert pale with fear, for a catastrophe loomed before us.[5]

It is difficult today to share these figures' sense of the strangeness and newness of *Tabula Rasa*, so integral has the sound of *tintinnabuli* become to the soundscape of the mediated present. But *Tabula Rasa* can still unsettle modes of hearing to which many, maybe most listeners are accustomed, and this chapter will consider some of the ways in which it does this. These include the work's use of musical sounds as frames for recurring stretches of silence and its generation of melodic material through the unfolding of algorithmic processes. They also include the work's sounding of a melodic line played at different speeds simultaneously, and its synthesis of a distinct sound world from a disparate array of gestures and idioms—what Schnittke would have called its polystylism. The goal of this chapter is not to explain how Pärt himself understands *Tabula Rasa*, though I will make frequent references to his perspectives. Neither is it to provide a comprehensive account of the work's unfolding. Rather, it is to suggest some ways in which we might make sense of the piece in relation to some of the other sounds and ideas that have shaped the worlds in which it has circulated—its silences pointing to American experimentalism and to the ascetic practices of his Orthodox Christian faith; the temporal unfolding of its structures inflecting experiences of electronically mediated sound; and its stylistic eclecticism recalling and refracting histories of Western classical music, and the history of Pärt's own journey as well.

SILENCE

The piece begins with the violin soloists playing a pair of As, four octaves apart and at maximum volume, followed by a measure of silence marked "G.P." in the score: "grand pause," *all quiet* (figure 4.3). Upon first hearing, this opening gesture might sound like the beginnings of many other works of Classical music, as it stakes out the home key of the piece in the most unadorned of ways (think of the opening of Beethoven's Third Symphony, for instance). But as Lothar Mattner strikingly put it just as *Tabula Rasa* was becoming

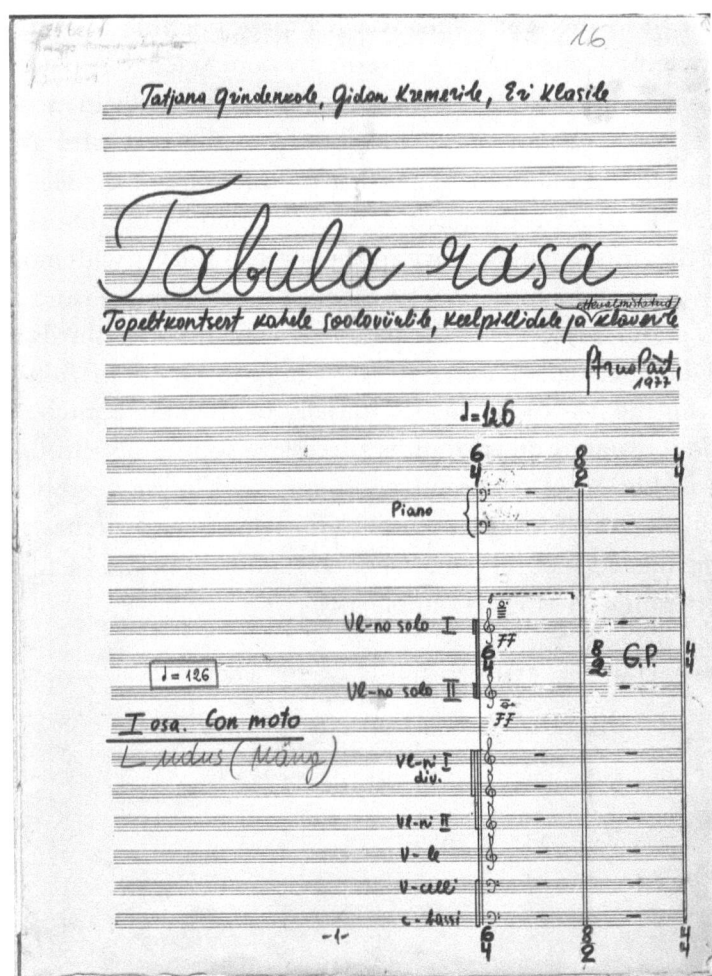

FIGURE 4.3 First page of the autograph score. Estonian Theatre and Music Museum, M238:2/8; and Arvo Pärt Centre. Used by permission.

known in the West, already with these opening bars "the whole first movement is essentially concluded."[6] After the silence of measure 2, the pitch A sounds repeatedly in measures 3–10, shadowed by T-voices from the orchestra and soloists and followed by another full measure of silence. In measures 12–24, the pitch A is augmented by neighboring pitches immediately above and below it (B and G), with more T-voices and another bar of silence observed in measure 25 (▶ audio 4.1). So goes the pattern for the first two thirds of *Ludus* (in English: *Play*), the opening movement of *Tabula Rasa*: the M-voice consists initially of the single pitch A, and it expands on each of its successive soundings through the addition of consecutively higher and lower neighboring pitches. T-voices sound from soloists and orchestra, and silence is observed after each statement of the steadily expanding M-voice (example 4.1).

EXAMPLE 4.1   First three iterations of the expanding M-voice in *Ludus*.

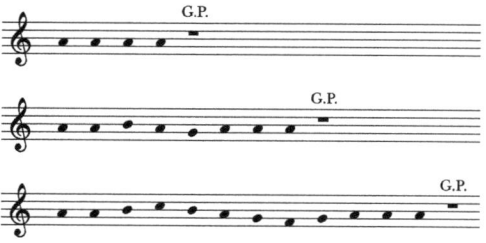

As Mattner suggests, nearly the whole of *Ludus* can be heard as a gradual expansion of (or variation on) the simple, even elemental idea expounded in its first two measures. Nothing really new appears, at least for the first two-thirds of the movement. Or, as Svetlana Savenko argues, the first two measures of the movement might be considered to contain the germ of *Tabula Rasa* as a whole. For that opening idea—a single pitch and a stretch of silence—is perhaps the most essential idea expressible in the language of Western music. And *tabula rasa*, as she notes, "means 'blank slate' in Latin—that is, 'from nothing,' *ab ovo*."[7]

Naturally, attention is drawn to the sounds of the soloists and the orchestra: to the otherworldly clang of the prepared piano, and to the gradual expansion of the M-voice over the course of the movement. But the score of *Ludus* might also be regarded the other way around, with its sounding passages providing a frame for the silences in between them. As Pärt has remarked on many occasions, to prepare the listener for the experience of silence is, in his view, one of his cardinal projects as composer. He asks: "How can one fill the time with notes worthy of the preceding silence?" And: "How can one fill the stillness (the silence) to come, with tones worthy of the silence (the stillness) that came before?"[8] For Pärt, to regard the composer's task as the creation of musical frames for silence—musical frames that prepare us to receive or listen for silence—is to invite the listener's contemplation of God and the miracle of creation. "When I speak of silence," he confided to the musicologist Ulrich Mosch, "I mean this 'nothing' from which God created the world. For that reason, rests are holy, regarded ideally."[9] To open his work to silence, Pärt suggests, is to leave space for reflection on, and maybe hearing of, something larger and higher than the self and the sounds the composer creates. On this point, his words recall lines of thinking about the place of sound and singing in Orthodox worship, and about the so-called *hesychastic* tradition—of "prayer in inner silence"—that informs much of Orthodox practice.[10] As Engelhardt has written of musical practice in the Orthodox Church of Estonia, "as a form of Orthodox sound, silence is the truth within which prayer and participation in the life of God (*theosis*) become possible."[11] Or, as the Orthodox scholar Peter C. Bouteneff writes, "Knowing God ensures stability of life. And the way to that knowledge is through quiet…. Before one talks about the ultimate goal of 'solidarity and union with God in *hesychia*' one must actually work to be emptied of inner noise."[12] One must become silent.

But there is something else to be said of the silence that resounds in *Tabula Rasa*, since for any composer to speak of his or her music as a frame for silence is also to point (unavoidably, even if unintentionally) to the legacy of John Cage, whose music and writings were central to shaping the philosophies and soundscapes of much of the postwar avant-garde. In *Tabula Rasa*, the specter of Cage is conjured all the more powerfully by the sound of the prepared piano, an instrument—really a modification of the traditional grand piano, achieved by inserting screws or other objects between its strings—that Cage invented around 1940 and made famous with his *Sonatas and Interludes* and other works of that decade. The fact that Pärt's use of the prepared piano was inspired by Schnittke in this case does nothing to weaken the association. The extent of Pärt's familiarity with Cage prior to his emigration is uncertain. But Cage's music was discussed in Soviet circles, even official ones, as early as 1959, and it was performed in Moscow, Riga, and elsewhere in the union with some frequency in the 1960s and 70s.[13] One particular work by Cage figures prominently in a pair of Schnittke's theoretical essays from the 1970s: Cage's famous "silent" piece from 1952, entitled *4′33″*.[14] That work, widely regarded as the archetype of a musical composition conceived as a frame for silence, consists simply of a performer sitting onstage for the prescribed duration without playing her instrument.

In Cage's view, *4′33″* had a didactic purpose. It served to demonstrate that absolute silence does not exist in the world, to help its audiences appreciate that "something is always happening that makes a sound." It served, in short, to teach its listeners to *listen*, not only to music, but to the world.[15] For Cage, to open one's work to silence—to this pregnant silence, filled with sounds uncreated by the composer—was to step outside one's creative ego and yield to something higher and larger than the self. He expressed this view in a manner not far removed from Pärt's own way of speaking, though without the frame of Pärt's Christian faith. To open one's composition to silence, Cage wrote, is to open "the doors of the music to the sounds that happen to be in the environment," a move that entails a "psychological turning [that] leads to the world of nature, where, gradually or suddenly, one sees that humanity and nature, not separate, are in this world together."[16] It is to "give up the desire to control sound," to humble oneself before something larger than the self, to create amidst "the realization that we possess nothing."[17] Once, in conversation with Enzo Restagno, Pärt acknowledged his kinship with Cage with respect to their views of silence. When Restagno observed that "the silence between sounds is of the utmost importance," Pärt replied: "This reminds me of something I said earlier that comes very close to the thinking of John Cage.

I don't remember it precisely, but I would put it more or less like this: 'How can one fill the stillness—the silence—to come, with tones worthy of the silence—the stillness—that came before?' There is no doubt: rests are full of sound."[18]

PROCESS

As shown in example 4.1, the M-voice of *Ludus* is generated by means of what we might call an iterative algorithmic process. It starts out as a single pitch (A), and it expands with each successive sounding by adding pitches directly above and below the highest and lowest pitches of the iteration that sounded immediately prior. Beginning on A, the M-voice commences its gradual expansion by adding the B above and the G below it. Then the M-voice expands again by adding the C above the B and the F below the G (▶ audio 4.1). Early on in his creation of *Ludus*, Pärt designed the algorithm by which the M-voice is generated. In a sketch for the work preserved in the archives, he worked out eight iterations of its expansion. He chose the initial input into the algorithm (the opening pitch A), and then, to borrow words from the music theorist Thomas Robinson, he *set the machine in motion*. Once the pitch A is plugged into the system, its iterative process generates, on its own, the movement's ever expanding M-voice.[19] Pärt used a variant of this same algorithmic process to generate the M-voice in the second movement, *Silentium* (*Silence*). There, starting with the initial pitch D, the M-voice begins its gradual expansion by ascending one pitch above and descending one pitch below that D. Then the M-voice continues to expand by ascending two pitches above D and falling two pitches below it, and so on (example 4.2, ▶ audio 4.2).

EXAMPLE 4.2   *Silentium*, mm. 1–7, cello part, showing the start of the iterative expansion of the M-voice.

The idea of generating pitch material by way of an algorithmic or autonomous process did not originate with Pärt. Rather, it reaches back, once again, to the postwar Western avant-garde: to the random processes Cage designed to generate material for his compositions beginning in the 1950s, and to the mathematical methods Boulez devised to compose his serial works of those same years.[20] In contrast to the work of those composers, however, the generative processes Pärt employs do not operate behind the scenes, as it were, generating pitch material out of earshot. Rather, they are immediately apprehensible to the listener—even, in the case of *Silentium*, upon one's very first hearing of the work. In this respect, Pärt's method seems more closely aligned with experiments undertaken by Steve Reich in America at almost exactly the same time, though neither Reich nor Pärt would become aware of each other's work until much later. (Some of Pärt's earlier compositions also derive their pitch material from this kind of audible generative process: *Modus* and *Calix*, for instance, both of which were performed in October 1976, and also *Solfeggio* of 1964, discussed in chapter 2.)[21]

In 1965 Reich composed *It's Gonna Rain*, the first in a series of process-driven works he would create over the next few years. In its entirety, the piece consists of a tape recording of a preacher played back on several loops of tape simultaneously, loops that are gradually allowed to fall out of sync with one another as the piece progresses. In this way, as Reich observed, the work exemplifies "pieces of music that are, literally, processes." He recounted his experience of composing them: "Although I may have the pleasure of discovering musical processes and composing the musical material to run through them, once the process is set up and loaded it runs by itself."[22] Reich's principal concern was that the unfolding of the process be immediately apprehensible to the listener, so that the "compositional process and [the] sounding music . . . are one and the same thing." He framed his experiments in contrast to Cage's algorithmic works, where "the compositional processes and the sounding music have no audible connection."[23] And yet, like Pärt's, Reich's distance from Cage was not so far philosophically. For whereas process, for Cage, was yet another means (like silence and chance) to separate his creator-ego from the product of his labors (to surrender to "the world of nature," as he put it), and whereas God, in Pärt's view, animates all that sounds in his music, so too did Reich link his interest in process to his desire to connect to something above or beyond human ego and life. He called that something, simply, *it*. "While performing and listening to gradual musical processes," he reflected, "one can participate in a particular liberating and impersonal kind of ritual. Focusing in on the musical process makes possible that shift of attention away from *he* and *she* and *you* and *me* outward toward *it*."[24]

For the critic Patrick Giles, *Tabula Rasa* constitutes a "23-minute meditation on the constant yet often barely perceptible progress of time," a perception that might owe something to the invariable rate at which the process of generating its M-voices unfolds. In *Silentium* that rate is approximately one quarter note per second, in time with a ticking clock.[25] But there is something else about *Silentium* in particular that might contribute to this impression. Namely, one of the hallmarks of its generative process is that each iteration of the M-voice's unfolding is longer than the preceding iteration by exactly four notes (see example 4.2). And one of the most salient features of Pärt's score is his signaling, with a D minor arpeggio flourish from the prepared piano, the arrival of every pitch D that the first solo violin plays as he or she unfolds the M-voice (example 4.3).

EXAMPLE 4.3   *Silentium*, mm. 1–5, prepared piano and first solo violin.

In each of the soloist's iterations of the M-voice, the piano flourish occurs exactly twice: once at its beginning, when D is first sounded, and once at its halfway point, as the melodic line returns from its ascent and begins its mirror-image descending motion (▶ audio 4.2). At first, these flourishes occur frequently. The first three flourishes in the movement (mm. 1–5) are separated by only two measures, establishing what one might readily, even reflexively perceive as a steady rhythm. But then, with the lengthening of the M-voice, the pacing of the flourishes slows audibly: first to every four measures (mm. 5–13), then to every six measures (mm. 13–25), then to every eight (mm. 25–41), and so on. Soon, the once audible rhythm of the recurring flourishes stretches to the point where we no longer hear them as regularly recurring at all—even, perhaps, to the point where we are no longer able to anticipate their return (figure 4.4).

In an influential book, the philosopher Jerrold Levinson suggests that many listeners make sense of what they hear by focusing on the discrete events or "individual parts" of a musical performance unfolding in time, rather than trying to apprehend a composition's large-scale structures or formal designs. In particular, he suggests, what a listener perceives as the coherence of a work is due to her ability to hear "the connections of such [individual] parts with immediately preceding and succeeding parts."[26] Although he writes only about tonal music, Levinson's theory of listening seems apt in the case of *Silentium*, since the percussive sound of

measure: 1 3 5   9   13   19   25   33   41   51   61   73   85   99   [...]

FIGURE 4.4   Spacing of piano flourishes in *Silentium*.

the prepared piano so readily draws the listener's attention to the rhythm of its flourishes amidst the otherwise undifferentiated sonic texture of the strings. We *hear* the piano's rhythm established at the beginning of the movement, and we *hear* it slow down over the course of subsequent measures. Significantly, Levinson notes that most listeners can perceive the unfolding connections between parts of a work only when they follow each other within a fairly short span of time, which "rarely exceeds a minute." Beyond that span, our aural attention simply becomes too saturated with the accumulation of discrete impressions to make instantaneous connections between present and past events.[27] In *Silentium*, with its steady tempo of one quarter note per second, and with its unchanging meter of six quarter notes to the bar, that one-minute threshold is reached just after measure 41, approximately a quarter of the way through the movement (see figure 4.4). It is as if the rhythm established at the beginning by the recurring flourish from the prepared piano recedes before our ears and eyes, slowing audibly and then passing beyond the limits of our hearing altogether. After measure 41 the flourish resurfaces only occasionally and probably unexpectedly, as if to remind us of a rhythm or pulse that used to be.

TECHNOLOGIES

The polyphonic structure of *Silentium* consists of the M-voice unfolding simultaneously at three different speeds, with each of those unfoldings shadowed by T-voices. As shown in example 4.4, the cellos play the M-voice in quarter notes and half notes. The orchestra's first violins play it in half notes and whole notes, and the first solo violin performs the M-voice as double whole notes (or a dotted whole note plus a half note, for a duration of eight quarters) and whole notes. In this way, the first violins expand the M-voice twice as rapidly as the soloist does, and the cellos unfold it twice as quickly as the first violins (▶ audio 4.2).

EXAMPLE 4.4   *Silentium*, mm. 1–5, showing the M-voice unfolding at three different speeds simultaneously.

Many of Pärt's early *tintinnabuli* works find their polyphonic textures in this way, by sounding an M-voice at two or more speeds simultaneously: *Calix*, for instance, as well as *Arbos* and *Cantus in Memory of Benjamin Britten*, both from 1977. Pärt calls the technique "proportional canon" (*Proportionskanon*), after a manner of composing in the Renaissance where two or more voices perform a single line at different speeds according to a fixed ratio.[28]

And yet, what Pärt composed in *Tabula Rasa* is not a proportional canon of the earlier kind, since the art of writing such a canon traditionally consisted in crafting a melodic line that, when played against itself at a different speed, yields a predominance of consonant intervals, and dissonances that are prepared and resolved in accordance with stylistic norms of polyphonic writing. In *Silentium*, the M-voice is not crafted in such a way at all. Instead, it is generated automatically, by way of the algorithm described earlier, and its sounding at three different speeds together gives rise to some highly dissonant textures, like those seen in example 4.4. In Pärt's work, and in stark contrast to earlier practice, the moment-to-moment juxtapositions of pitches are neither planned nor controlled. Rather, they derive from what might be called the *experiment*—again in a sense anticipated by Cage—of running a generative algorithmic process at three different rates simultaneously.[29]

It is likely that Pärt encountered examples of proportional canon in the early music he studied since the 1960s, and also in the repertoires performed by Andres Mustonen and Hortus Musicus. But the technique he employs in *Silentium* is, I think, more closely akin to Reich's in *It's Gonna Rain*, where a single tape recording of a spoken text is played back at several different speeds at once, the musical interest deriving from the unfolding of the experiment itself: from seeing (or hearing) what unplanned results are generated through such a procedure. Like Pärt, Reich pointed to the distant kinship between his work and the proportional canons of earlier ages, describing *It's Gonna Rain* "as an extension of the idea of infinite canon or round."[30] I also think that the distinctive mediality of Reich's experiment in *It's Gonna Rain*—an experiment made possible only through the affordance of electronic media—can be illuminating with respect to Pärt's composition. Of course, *Silentium* is not a work of electronic music, beyond the amplification of its prepared piano, and Pärt does not compose on a computer. But I think that the kind of texture in which it consists—the kind of sound experiment *Silentium* embodies—might well reflect ways of listening and manipulating sound that are indebted to the experience of music mediated electronically, and to the experiments with sound afforded by that mediation, which conditioned the experience in turn.

As the media theorist Friedrich Kittler points out, the ability to stretch or compress the length of a musical performance (what he calls "time-axis manipulation") was celebrated as a defining feature of phonographic recording from the time of its commercial debut, precisely because it promised a wholly unprecedented experience for listeners. From the earliest days of their production, gramophones were constructed so as to enable their users to vary the playback speed of records—either slightly, resulting in subtle changes of pitch, or drastically, enabling one to hear a melody twice as quickly or twice as slowly as it originally sounded.[31] The magnetic tape used in *It's Gonna Rain* combines this capacity for time-axis manipulation with the ability to layer sounds on top of each other in ways unattainable by other means prior to the advent of digital processing. As the musician and producer Brian Eno observed in 1979, the possibilities afforded by such "multitrack" recording and playback inspired whole new ways of thinking about composing, whether or not the music composed was electronic. With the advent of multitrack technology, Eno suggests, "you got an additive approach to recording, [and] the idea that the composition is the process of adding more.... You can begin to think in terms of putting something on, putting something else on, trying this on top of it, and so on.... In a compositional sense this takes the making of music away from any traditional way that composers worked ... and one becomes empirical in a way that the classical composer never was."[32]

The experience of working with sound electronically was not new to Pärt in 1977. Rather, it had been integral to his work as a musician since his student years. For a decade beginning in the 1950s, he worked as an engineer at Estonian Radio, where, amidst a crew of other technologically minded artists, he recorded performances, produced live broadcasts, and delved into the station's archive of recordings of music by the Western avant-garde (figure 4.5).[33] During and

FIGURE 4.5   Pärt at the control board of Estonian Radio, photographed by Valdur-PeeterVahi,1963.EstonianFilmArchives,fotonr.0-305704.Usedby permission.

after his time at the studio, Pärt was active, even prolific, as a composer of film scores, which provided him room to experiment in ways that were otherwise impossible in the USSR.[34] Pärt has often stressed that this work provided him with little more than a needed paycheck, but several films on which he worked in the 1970s exemplify ways of layering sounds that multitrack tape recording technologies afforded. These include the Russian-language crime drama *Diamonds for the Dictatorship of the Proletariat* (1975), which features passages like one that layers blaring locomotive horns atop ostinato figures played by piano, harp, and triangle.[35] And they include *Colorful Dreams* (1974), an hour-long film, largely devoid of dialogue, about a deeply imaginative young girl, in which the layering of contrasting or uncoordinated sound materials echoes her inability to accommodate to her world. Against scenes of the sea glimpsed from a rural fishing village, a girl's voice sings in the manner of a folk or nursery song, overlaid with aggressive rhythmic chanting and percussion in an unrelated tempo. Later, the girl's folk-like singing sounds above a rhythmic passage played by a vibraphone, once again in an unrelated tempo. When the girl's mother compels her to return to their apartment in the city, a recording of a child's crying and whispering is juxtaposed with what sounds like an early version of Pärt's *Modus* played on a harpsichord.[36] All of these passages reveal experiments—whether by Pärt or by a collaborating sound editor—with composition as a "process of adding more," in Eno's words: building up a musical texture by playing back several segments of tape simultaneously. Pärt's experiment with overlaying voices in *Tabula Rasa* might well reveal this same creative sensibility, brought to bear upon more traditional musical materials.

Here again, we come face to face with questions of time and its perception in Pärt's music. For as Leopold Brauneiss observes with reference to *Festina Lente* (1990), another of Pärt's compositions to feature multispeed layering of M-voices, "as the melody proceeds fast and slow at the same time, the fastest voice always sounds at the same time as its own stretched past."[37] But more than that, the ability to record music, to play it back, and to shorten or lengthen its time axis has always been couched in discourse on the capacity to "store" time, in Kittler's words, with time itself now experienced "as a mixture of audio frequencies in the acoustic realm." In the view of Charles Cros, a nineteenth-century inventor of the idea of the phonograph, the appeal of the technology consisted in its promise to halt time's previously inexorable flow: "Time would flee, I would subdue it."[38] In fact, as Jonathan Sterne observes, "if there was a defining figure in early accounts of sound recording, it was the possibility of preserving the voice beyond the death of the speaker."[39] Sterne's words bring us back to the critical tropes of stillness and timelessness considered at the beginning of this book, to statements about the ability of Pärt's music to "bind the mind to an eternal present," about Pärt's alleged propensity to compose "as if the history of music were at an end."[40] In light of the technologies of sound reproduction to which its multitrack layering of M-voices might point, and against the backdrop of Pärt's melodies sounding amidst present echoes of their own stretched pasts, we might hear *Silentium* as a meditation on the promise of mediated sound itself, on the possibility of preserving a voice beyond history, beyond death.

PASTS

Early listeners to *Tabula Rasa* were often struck by what Schnittke would have called its polystylistic quality. "Neo-baroque" is how a Polish writer described it after hearing it performed at the Warsaw Autumn festival in 1978.[41] "Vivaldi with a scream" is what a critic from New York wrote of a performance of 1986. In an essay published in the *Frankfurter allgemeine Zeitung* in 1984, the critic Wolfgang Sandner suggested that "the icons of earlier times and the sounds of today are combined in his music: John Cage's prepared piano and the violin parts from Vivaldi's *Four Seasons*."[42] As a British writer put it the previous year, *Tabula Rasa* struck her as a "chameleon-like work, which so closely mirrors the style of the Italian Baroque string composers that on casual hearing it seems more closely related to pastiche than to original composition."[43]

As we saw in chapter 2, Schnittke coined the term *polystylism* (in Russian, *polistilistika*) sometime around 1970, partly in response to Pärt's collagelike compositions of the previous decade. However, Schnittke also found inspiration in Pärt's works that do not make use of direct quotations, but exhibit instead "more subtle ways of using elements of another's style" in his own. Schnittke found an example of that subtler technique in Pärt's *Pro et Contra*, a concerto composed in 1966 for the cellist Mstislav

Rostropovich. As Schnittke heard it, *Pro et Contra* does not quote directly from any specific predecessor, but finds its "parodic foundation" (*parodiinaia opora*) in more generic aspects of style—specifically, in "cadential formulas from the Baroque."[44] If, like Sandner, one hears echoes of Cage and Vivaldi in *Tabula Rasa*, one will search in vain for literal quotations from works by those composers. Rather, as in the case of *Pro et Contra*, those echoes will derive from the sounding traces of what Schnittke called the "scents and shadows of other times" pervading this corner of Pärt's work.[45]

In some ways, it is unsurprising that *Tabula Rasa* would make play of such scents and shadows, for Pärt's discovery of *tintinnabuli* left untouched his long-standing interest in polystylistic composition, as attested in *If Bach Had Kept Bees*. But there might have been a specific impetus toward polystylism in the case of *Tabula Rasa*, since when Kremer and Grindenko approached him about composing something for the duo, they sought a companion piece to Schnittke's First Concerto Grosso, which vividly demonstrates a quality Schnittke called "stylistic polyphony" (*stilisticheskaia polifoniia*).[46] Schnittke's concerto opens with what he described as a "lively children's chorale," albeit one rendered by the prepared piano, denatured in its timbre by the insertion of bolts between its strings, and performed at such a slow tempo as to give it the quality of a funeral dirge—"sounding like a cross between Radio Moscow's signature chimes and the beating of ash cans," one critic suggested (▶ audio 4.3).[47] In the concerto's second movement, titled "Toccata," quick, tonal-sounding figures from the soloists alternate with tonally static echoes in the orchestra and passages for soloists and harpsichord that sound like they could have been taken straight from a Vivaldi concerto, if it were not for the highly dissonant orchestral writing that follows. "Genuine Corelli," Schnittke wrote of the movement, referring to Arcangelo Corelli, an Italian master of the Baroque concerto, only "made in the USSR." The fifth movement, a rondo, features sustained imitative writing for the soloists, who trade a snappy tonal figure above a harpsichord that delivers an over-the-top, romantic rendering of a Baroque figured bass (▶ audio 4.4). Soon, the entire ensemble yields to a tango—"a tango beloved by my grandmother, which her great grandmother played on the harpsichord"—and a recap of the prepared piano "children's chorale" of the concerto's beginning.[48] As Schnittke explained, he regarded his concerto as an attempt at "overcoming the gap between *E* and *U*"—those being, in Schnittke's mix of German and Russian, *Ernst* or "serious music" and *Unterhaltung* or "light music" (*razvlekatel'naia muzyka*). He sought to bring "fragments" of such musics together not in a "humorous way, but as elements of a diverse musical reality."[49]

The polystylism of Schnittke's concerto was deliberately historicizing. It consisted in sounding together the historical traces of a complex contemporary soundscape, and in making audible the multiple pasts that collectively shaped the world he addressed. The same, I think, can be said of *Tabula Rasa*, though its sound could hardly be more different from that of Schnittke's work. First, there are the shadows of Cage, circa 1948, cast by Pärt's use of the prepared piano. Then there is the genre of the concerto itself, and especially the style of concerto writing honed by Corelli and Vivaldi in the seventeenth and eighteenth centuries. One of the functions of the genre was to provide a platform for virtuosic display by one or more soloists, set against and often in opposition to the massed players of the orchestra. In a typical concerto of the Italian Baroque, passages for soloists alternate with "ritornello" passages from the orchestra. The ritornello evolves over the course of a movement, but it always retains enough similarity to the original as to be immediately recognizable at every return.[50] Throughout the first movement of *Tabula Rasa*, Pärt maintains a version of this structure. Each statement of the expanding M-voice (example 4.1) begins with a canonic passage played by the orchestra. That passage yields to a highly ornamented unfolding of the M-voice by the soloists, who yield in turn to another canonic passage from the orchestra. Then, silence is ushered in with bell-like clanging from the prepared piano. This basic pattern (orchestra–soloists–orchestra–piano–silence) structures every statement of the M-voice (▶ audio 4.1). The soloists' ornamentation of the M-voice likewise echoes Vivaldi's writing, consisting of quick, arpeggio figures articulating pitches of the T-voice above and below the M-voice.

The coalescence of the concerto genre around the turn of the eighteenth century is often regarded as an important moment in the development of tonality itself, by virtue of its sometimes elaborate play with cycles of harmonic tension and release. Moreover, the genre's setting of individual musicians (soloists) apart from or in opposition to the united forces of a group (the orchestra) "suggest[ed] a social paradigm or metaphor," as Taruskin describes it, or "a kind of microcosm, a model of social interaction and coordinated (or competitive) activity."[51] Both of these technical features—novelties around 1700—combined to lend the Italian concerto a palpable and unprecedented sense of drama. Of course, *Tabula Rasa* is not a tonal work, and Kremer recalled being dumbstruck by its harmonic stasis when he first laid eyes on its score. But at a decisive moment approximately three-quarters of the way through its first movement, Pärt brought elements of the drama of the Baroque concerto directly into play by breaking suddenly and jarringly with *tintinnabuli* technique.

At measure 192 in *Ludus*, at a point marked "cadenza" in the published score (though not in the autograph manuscript or extant sketches), Pärt arrests the algorithmic expansion of the M-voice with a loud, slow, stepwise, three-octave descent from the piano, the soloists, and the orchestra's first violins and cellos (▶ audio 4.5).[52] Then, at measure 214, in a dramatic assertion of a composerly subject over the autonomous processes that have unfolded to that point, the system of *tintinnabuli* is shattered. What Pärt gives us, sounding at full volume and for two full bars, is a diminished seventh chord (spelled D♯, F♯, A, C), a chord that includes two pitches (D♯ and F♯) that cannot be generated by the algorithm used to expand the M-voice, and that do not belong to the movement's A minor triadic space of *tintinnabuli* (example 4.5).

EXAMPLE 4.5 *Ludus*, m. 214, orchestral parts.

At measure 216 the piano bangs out an A minor triad, as if to insist on the pitches that sounded constantly until just a moment ago. But right after that, on the second beat of that bar, the orchestra plays the diminished chord again. With that second sounding of the diminished chord, however, an A minor triad sounds subtly within it, as the violas add an E♮ to the mass of dissonant pitches. In measures 218 and 220 the piano continues to insist on A minor, while the orchestra's response gives increasing prominence to the A minor triad enveloped within the dissonant collection of tones. In measure 218 the root of the orchestra's dissonant chord was a C, but in measure 220 it switches to A. Finally, by the fourth beat of measure 222, the triadic space of *tintinnabuli* is restored. The transgressing pitches of the diminished chord are silenced, leaving only the A minor triad (example 4.6, ▶ audio 4.6).

EXAMPLE 4.6 *Ludus*, harmonic structure of mm. 214–22, with the A minor triad emerging within and finally supplanting the dissonant, diminished chord.

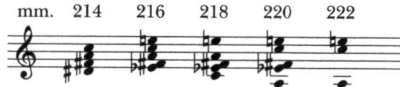

For four more measures the orchestra plays that triad loudly and aggressively, until the movement closes abruptly with unison As, played throughout the ensemble.

To describe the effect of the end of *Ludus* in the dramatic, "social" terms of the concerto genre, one might say that a crisis or disruption of the movement's stable unfolding occurs at the point in the score marked "cadenza" (m. 192). That crisis allows an intruder—the diminished chord—to threaten the very foundations of the sound world previously established in the movement: its algorithmically generated M-voice and its mirror in the triadic space of *tintinnabuli*. But then, over the course of those measures described in example 4.6, the piano's steadfast insistence on A minor gains support in the orchestra's strings, which eventually succeed in stamping out the vitality of the adversary, forcefully silencing and expelling the intruder just before the movement's end. If *tintinnabuli* is regarded as a sounding experience of harmony or tranquility, then peace is restored at the end of this movement only through violent overcoming, even exclusion.

The drama of *Ludus* is wholly of a kind with what we encounter in concertos by Vivaldi, where prominently articulated, distant key areas often threaten to unsettle a movement's tonal center, which is reestablished only by excluding the foreign harmonies from the work. The drama of *Ludus* is likewise consistent with the polystylisic allegory of Schnittke's First Concerto Grosso, with its "easily read contrasts" in which "discord, heard always as the opposite or absence of concord, functions as a sign."[53] But then again, such stark and dramatically suggestive contrasts had been hallmarks of Pärt's music for over a decade: since *Credo*, which opposed Bach's bright C major with dodecaphony and aleatoric cacophony, and since *Collage über B–A–C–H*, which played Bach's sarabande against chromatic clusters of notes. As Sandner suggested, there are many pasts that circulate and resound in *Tabula Rasa*. There is the past of Cage and the postwar avant-garde, of Reich and the history of electronic sound reproduction, of Vivaldi and Corelli and the dramatic concerto of the Italian Baroque. But there is also the past of Pärt himself—of the dramatic gestures that sustained his music and career in their formative and most highly experimental periods, amidst the ever-present hazards of the social and political worlds in which he had no choice but to subsist. If *Tabula Rasa* reconfigures musically aspects of the classical tradition, so too does it reclaim and refashion aspects of its composer's own creative journey, lived within the Soviet Union, yet also within the expansive boundaries of a West that was, at that point, still largely imagined.[54]

The ending of *Silentium* is famous. After unfolding eight expansions of the M-voice, the piano, soloists, and members of the orchestra fall silent one by one, leaving only the contrabasses to continue their downward tracing of the voice's arc. As the instruments drop out, the sound of the ensemble grows quieter, the texture sparser. Finally, the contrabasses reach the lowest pitch playable on the instrument without modification by a special extension. That lowest pitch is an E, so the descending line of the M-voice stops one note shy of the D that a tonally conditioned listener would expect to hear in order to perceive closure in the work. At that point, *Tabula Rasa* ceases to sound, dissolving into silence. The effect of these final moments is not unlike that of the "fade" ending that closes much electronically created music, especially rock. As Eno writes, the fade "implies not that the piece has finished but that it is *continuing out of earshot* . . . that the music is a section from a hypothetical continuum."[55]

When *Tabula Rasa* was premiered alongside Schnittke's First Concerto Grosso on September 30, 1977, in the auditorium of the Tallinn Polytechnic Institute (today's Tallinn University), the quiet, ambiguous close of the work left its audience speechless, unwilling to move and disturb the silence, unsure if it had really ended at all (figure 4.6). "I have never since felt such silence in the hall" as at the end of that first performance, recalled Nora Pärt. "The silence was so stunning," the composer remembered, "that people were almost afraid to breathe!"[56] One report in the Estonian press on the concert was understated: "*Tabula Rasa* made a profound impression on the audience."[57] But another was emphatic, even visually so, leaving a blank space on the page as a testament to the silence into which *Silentium* dissolved:

A. Pärt's *Tabula Rasa* is . . .

. . .

Those who heard it need no verbal description—which, after all, would be of pretty much no help whatsoever. To those who

ПРОГРАММА

I

ИОГАНН СЕБАСТИАН БАХ (1685—1750) — Концерт для двух скрипок и оркестра ре минор BWV 1043

1. Vivace
2. Largo ma non tanto
3. Allegro

АРВО ПЯРТ (1935) — «Tabula rasa», двойной концерт для двух скрипок, струнных и подготовленного рояля (первое исполнение)

Посвящается Татьяне Гринденко, Гидону Кремеру и Эри Класу

1. Con moto
2. Senza moto

II

ФРАНЦ ШУБЕРТ (1797—1828) — Полонез си-бемоль мажор для скрипки и маленького оркестра

Солист —
ГИДОН КРЕМЕР

АЛЬФРЕД ШНИТКЕ (1934) — Concerto grosso для двух скрипок, подготовленного рояля, клавесина и струнных

Посвящается Татьяне Гринденко, и Гидону Кремеру

1. Preludio
2. Toccata
3. Recitativo
4. Cadenza
5. Rondo
6. Postludio

FIGURE 4.6 Program for the premiere of *Tabula Rasa*, September 30, 1977, with Tatiana Grindenko, Gidon Kremer, and the RAT Estonia Chamber Orchestra conducted by Eri Klas at the Tallinn Polytechnic Institute. The concert also included J. S. Bach's D minor Concerto for Two Violins, BWV 1043; Schubert's B♭ major Polonaise; and Schnittke's First Concerto Grosso. The italicized text indicates that *Tabula Rasa* was "dedicated to Tatiana Grindenko, Gidon Kremer, and Eri Klas." Estonian Theatre and Music Museum, M238/1:4. Used by permission.

did not hear it, it is impossible to convey a sense of the glowing atmosphere that surrounded the performance.[58]

One month later, on October 27, Grindenko and Kremer brought *Tabula Rasa* to the Great Hall of the Leningrad Philharmonic, an event that seems to have generated no press.[59] But in his later memoirs, Kremer recalled the candid impressions of a ranking official in the Soviet Ministry of Culture. "A very good evening," Kremer remembered the official declaring shortly after the Tallinn premiere. "But do you really believe the public liked the work? You know, all this hysteria about the success"—the audience's ovations, Kremer explained—"might better be described as a political position. A highly questionable composer...."[60] As was the case after the scandalous premiere of *Credo* nine years earlier, once more Pärt's success was comprehensible to Soviet officialdom only as a political statement. Four weeks after their concert in Leningrad, the duo took *Tabula Rasa* on tour, performing it in Kiev, Riga, Munich, Leverkusen, Bonn, Cologne, Vienna, and Graz. In city after city in which they played, the success of the premiere was repeated. And with that, the composer's political difficulties became very real indeed.

CHAPTER 5
EXPORT AND EMIGRATION

IN NOVEMBER AND DECEMBER 1977, Kremer and Grindenko took *Tabula Rasa* on the road. Their companions in travel were the musicians of the Lithuanian Chamber Orchestra and its conductor, Saulius Sondeckis, and also Alfred Schnittke, for whom Kremer secured an exit visa by enlisting him as the ensemble's pianist. "Alfred was very nervous," Kremer recalled of the arrangement. "He hardly played in public."[1] Their tour was to last two months, sweeping through West Germany and Austria, with orchestral performances interspersed with recitals by the soloists. In addition to *Tabula Rasa* and Schnittke's First Concerto Grosso, the travelers' repertoire included

FIGURE 5.1 Tatiana Grindenko, Gidon Kremer, Alfred Schnittke, and the RAT Estonia Chamber Orchestra, conducted by Eri Klas, performing Schnittke's First Concerto Grosso at the Tallinn Polytechnic Institute, September 30, 1977. Schnittke is seated at the harpsichord. The first half of the concert featured the premiere of Pärt's *Tabula Rasa*. Arvo Pärt Centre. Used by permission.

Shostakovich's Chamber Symphony, op. 110a, Mozart's D major Divertimento, K. 136, and works by Schubert, J. S. Bach, and Henry Purcell (figure 5.1).

By the time of the tour, Kremer had become a familiar presence in the West, where he had appeared in festivals and competitions since the 1960s: in Brussels, Genoa, and Montreal. He had accompanied the Leningrad Symphony on its tour of Germany in 1975, and he soloed with the Berlin Philharmonic under Herbert von Karajan the following year.[2] For most of his companions, however, the journey provided a rare and even unprecedented glimpse of life beyond the eastern bloc. For Schnittke, who had spent part of his childhood in Vienna, it was his first trip outside the USSR in more than a quarter century.

Unbeknownst to his fellow musicians, Kremer had been plotting to use the occasion of the tour to ask—and to pressure—authorities in Moscow to grant him something extraordinary for a Soviet artist: permission to live and work abroad for two full years. "My intent was not defection," he remembered, "but a challenge."[3] While still in Moscow, he had addressed a letter to Petr Demichev, the Soviet Minister of Culture, asking for a two-year extension of his stay abroad, and he left the letter with a romantic partner, who had agreed to deliver it to the minister the moment she received Kremer's cue. "This request," Kremer's letter to Demichev read, "arises solely from my creative interests and has no political or other goals.... I hope that my activities abroad will foster a drawing together of cultures and a better understanding between peoples, and also of the humanistic tradition of our country."[4] When the tour arrived in the West German capital of Bonn in late November, he directed his partner to deliver his missive on the day he informed the Soviet ambassador of his plans to overstay his visa. For a time, Kremer remembers, it seemed certain that authorities would treat his request as a defection, which would have posed real dangers not only to him but to his family at home and his partners on tour. After days of ambiguous and sometimes ominous communications, the Ministry of Culture agreed to his request, provided that he first return to Moscow once the tour was completed. Kremer agreed, and Demichev kept his promise. Back in the Soviet capital, Kremer received official approval for a two-year sojourn on January 16, 1978. He flew to London that day.[5] It was a rare and perhaps unprecedented opening of spaces and opportunities to a Soviet musician.

Kremer's tour of 1977 enabled another historic opening as well: of Western audiences to *Tabula Rasa*, and to the sounds of Pärt's *tintinnabuli*. Although his music had occasionally featured in programs abroad since the 1960s, *Tabula Rasa* was among the first *tintinnabuli* compositions to be performed outside the USSR. Many of those who heard it on tour were confounded by what they experienced, captivated by its sounds while at a loss to account for its origins, coming as it did from an unfamiliar corner of northeastern Europe and from a composer whom most had never heard of before. In a review from Bonn, Pärt was misidentified as Russian, while in Graz he was identified as Finnish. The program for the group's concert in Leverkusen explained that he had composed the piece for Grindenko and Kremer, but that "no further information about *Tabula Rasa* is available to us."[6]

Nearly everywhere, the sound of Pärt's composition—with its silence and slowness, its melodic process and harmonic stasis, all sounding so different from the classical canon and the avant-garde alike—elicited comparisons with imaginary "Far Eastern" (*fernöstliche*) musics, and also with progressive rock. In Munich: "This is not an 'Indian' composer, as many listeners had understood (those who found the work to be Baroque-Indian), and he is no Silesian, as others believed, nor even a Saxon, but an 'Estonian.'" In Cologne: "In its expansiveness and extensive use of high and soft registers, this movement [*Silentium*] imparts a reflection of eternal rest. One can imagine it serving as a toehold into Far Eastern meditations."⁷ A critic from Bonn suggested that the impression of rest or stillness derives from "auditory effects the composer might have learned from highly skilled pop groups [*hochqualifizierter Pop-Gruppen*] with inclinations toward a Far Eastern mythos of sound." Apparently recalling the latter review, a concert program from Vienna explained: "In its graphic appearance, the second movement is reminiscent of the organum of the Notre Dame School of the thirteenth century. But with the gonglike coloration of the piano and its slowing of the tempo almost to the point of stasis, it attains a quality of mysticism or Far Eastern music, not unlike the effects of highly skilled pop groups such as Pink Floyd." A review of the same performance in Vienna called the work "psychedelic."[8]

In Bonn, it was reported, the audience sat breathlessly at the end of *Silentium* until "an enthusiastic storm of applause broke the silence"—echoing accounts in the Estonian press of the work's September premiere.[9] Calling *Tabula Rasa* a "fabulous" or "dreamlike" (*traumhaftes*) work, one Graz-based critic declared Pärt's composition the highlight of the concert, making for an "evening such as Graz rarely sees." He or she continued: "It's just a shame that this Estonian is not better known among us."[10] As it happened, the latter condition would soon be altered decisively, for the ensemble's Bonn concert of November 26 was co-sponsored by West German Radio,[11] which produced a recording that made its way to Manfred Eicher, the founder of ECM Records in Munich. Within in few years, and with Eicher's help, Pärt, *Tabula Rasa*, and *tintinnabuli* would become household names across Western Europe and beyond.

In the autumn of 1977, however, that turn of events was still some years off, and it was completely unimaginable. At home in Tallinn while Kremer was abroad, Pärt's life was becoming ever more complicated. On the one hand, *Tabula Rasa* was performed repeatedly throughout the Soviet Union and the eastern bloc: in Kiev in November, in Riga in January, in Kislovodsk in February, in Leningrad and Moscow in 1979.[12] In May 1978 the work earned Pärt the Award of the Year (*Aastapreemia*) from the Union of Soviet Estonian Composers. Four months later *Tabula Rasa* was programmed at the Warsaw Autumn Festival. In November it was performed at the Festival of Old and Contemporary Music in Tallinn (figure 5.2).[13] At the same time, Pärt's other

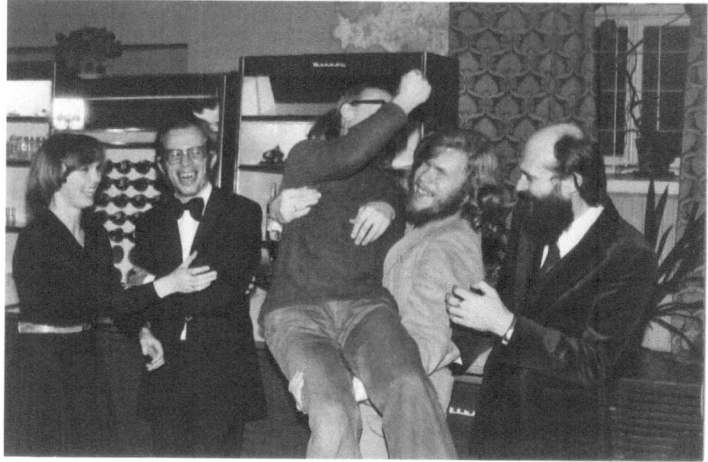

FIGURE 5.2 Pärt (*far right*) with friends at the Festival of Old and Contemporary Music in Tallinn, November 11, 1978: Tatiana Grindenko, Gidon Kremer, and Andres Mustonen holding the pianist Alexei Liubimov. Estonian Theatre and Music Museum, M238/1:11. Used by permission.

tintinnabuli works were beginning to garner considerable attention. In Leningrad and Tallinn, Mustonen and Hortus Musicus recapped versions of the 1976 *tintinnabuli* concert under the auspices of the cities' philharmonics, and they performed another version of the suite at the Leningrad House of Composers in December 1978. The previous year, Pärt's work had featured in a ten-day festival of Soviet music in East Germany.[14]

Another measure of Pärt's success was the warm reception his *tintinnabuli* works received among a new generation of Soviet musicians coming of age in the later 1970s, including the pianist Alexei Liubimov, the composer Vladimir Martynov, and the artist and DJ Hardijs Lediņš. Unlike Schnittke, Gubaidulina, and most others of Pärt's generation, Martynov recalled, Pärt had "succeeded in overcoming the gravitational pull of the avant-garde. Passing over the hill of serialism, aleatoric and sonoristic work, [he] arrived at a new tonal, or rather modal music." That music, for Martynov and many of his colleagues, was one whose harmonic stasis and textural clarity resonated with the sounds of their own creative experiments, and it reflected a kind of spiritual searching in which they themselves were engaged.[15] The popular embrace of Pärt's music in these years sometimes gave rise to remarkable events. In May 1978 the Georgia Philharmonic in Tbilisi even revived Pärt's notorious *Credo*, performing it under the heading *Fantasy in C Major* and accompanying the performance with a program note that quoted directly from the Nicene Creed.[16]

Following the popular reception of *Tabula Rasa* in Austria and West Germany, orchestras in other Western locales began programming Pärt's *tintinnabuli* music, and the composer started receiving invitations to attend rehearsals and concerts abroad. With these, however, came a series of increasingly difficult encounters with Soviet bureaucracy. For December 6, 1978, the British Broadcasting Corporation had planned a performance of *Cantus* in London, where Pärt was scheduled to appear. Two days before the concert, however, the Soviet conductor Kirill Kondrashin defected while touring Holland, and officials abruptly canceled Pärt's exit visa, wary of others following Kondrashin's lead. Dramatically, the *Guardian* announced the cancellation by proclaiming, in an essay quoted earlier in this book, "There are dissident Soviet composers too."[17] The following summer Pärt's request to attend a performance of *Tabula Rasa* at a festival in Kuhmo, Finland, was summarily denied.[18] "Usually, I didn't even know about invitations I'd received," he recalled in 1981. "The Composers' Union would decline in my name without even letting me know where and to what I'd been invited. They'd give some excuse like 'He has to finish a film score.' Sometimes, six or eight months later, I'd meet the person who invited me and he'd say 'Have you finished your film score yet?' And I'd say: 'What film score?' "[19]

As it happened, the late 1970s constituted a veritable season of defections and departures to the West by Soviet musicians. In addition to Kondrashin there was the pianist Youri Egorov, who defected in 1976, and the conductor Rudolf Barshai, who emigrated to Israel the following year. "It is the tragedy of our entire Russian intelligentsia," confided the pianist Mikhail Rudy shortly after his own defection to France in 1977. "The list is endless," Kremer remarked two years later.[20] In this climate, Kremer's uncertain loyalties and new residence abroad could only have made matters more difficult for Pärt. Beyond all of this, the composer recalled, there was the fact of his marriage to Nora, who was raised in a Jewish household and whose parents had, like Barshai, resettled in Israel. As he explained in 1987, "I married a young woman whose parents lived in Israel. Since Jews were permitted to leave the USSR, it seemed that I had publicly declared my intention to emigrate. For ten years I hung on. But I began to be known abroad. When I was invited to Finland or Canada, a visa was systematically refused to me."[21]

As Pärt told the journalist Anne Rey about this difficult period, there came a point in 1979 when his life in the USSR seemed to reach a dead end. Increasingly in demand outside the USSR, with new opportunities presenting themselves by the month, he was repeatedly confronted by the restriction or denial of those opportunities by officials at home, whose anxiety about his possible defection only increased as he became more famous in the West. Recounting his participation in a conference of composers in Tallinn in the winter of 1979, he recalled the breaking point as follows:

> On my way, I stopped at a movie studio and borrowed a wig, very long and very greasy. When my turn came to speak, I disappeared beneath the desk, put on my disguise, and stepped up to the podium: "What do you think I resemble?" The audience was petrified. I pulled out the page from the *Guardian* and proclaimed: "Read here, I am a dissident." I don't know how I avoided a trip to the psychiatric ward. There comes a time when you lose patience, when you're capable of saying everything that's on your mind over the telephone, which amounts

to shouting it out in a public place. In 1980, we arrived at that point. It seemed to us like everyone was arranging for our final departure. In three weeks, in record time, we received permission to emigrate.[22]

At this point in the story, I turn its recounting over to the composer and his wife:

> [Arvo:] The conduct toward me by people in the regime was the decisive factor. They made it clear that they would not be unhappy if my wife and I were to leave the country.... In their opinion, performances of my works abroad had become too frequent... The reviews of my works in the West were positive, but that only led to a worsening of my situation, which quickly became unbearable, for them and for me....
>
> [Nora:] In autumn, a leading member of the Central Committee visited us at home and recommended that we leave the country. It was meant to look like our own decision, but in reality it amounted to expulsion from the country, and it was irreversible.... After that visit we immediately began preparing the documents for our expatriation, because there was no possibility of staying any longer. Shortly afterward, Arvo was advised to resign from the Composers' Union.... When Arvo came home that day from the union he was paler than I have ever seen him.... It took two or three weeks for us to organize our departure and clear out our apartment.... We had no idea whatsoever where we could go, but we had no intention of going to Israel, the only country for which we'd been granted an exit visa.... There was no time for sentimentality or emotions. We had to go.... At five o'clock in the morning we got into two taxis in Tallinn, and we told our children we were embarking on a trip around the world, and that at the end of such journeys you always had to come back to where you started.[23]

They took a train to Brest-Litovsk on the Polish border, cleared customs, and boarded another bound for Vienna. As Nora recalled of the Austrian capital, "We knew that emigrants were to be brought together in a camp there, where they would await travel onward to Israel."[24]

On the morning of January 20, 1980, the composer and his family were met at a Vienna station by a representative of the historic publishing firm Universal Edition. The meeting might have been arranged by Schnittke, who, like a number of his Soviet colleagues, had worked with Universal since the 1960s. The representative offered to help the family find an apartment and apply for Austrian citizenship, and with that Pärt's enduring relationship with the publisher was cemented.[25] In conversation a few days later with a journalist from the Vienna daily *Die Presse*, Pärt was upbeat in a disorienting time, focusing intently on a series of concerts and commissions to which he had already committed, often with Soviet artists: "Natalia Gutman and Leonid Kogan are playing something by him, Gennady Rozhdestvensky has requested something for orchestra and also for piano duet, for Viktoria Postnikova and himself. There's a commission from the Helsinki Festival, and Gidon Kremer wants something for the Salzburg Festival in 1981."[26] One year later *Tabula Rasa* received its London premiere by the BBC Symphony Orchestra, and the ensemble Continuum soon began programming and promoting Pärt's *tintinnabuli* music in New York, often relying on scores sent secretly to its director by a friend in the USSR.[27]

Living abroad, Pärt encountered a West that differed radically from what he had imagined while living in Estonia, and he faced something he had not anticipated: the frequent, even reflexive pigeonholing of his music and public persona within broad yet vividly designated categories of music and creativity. This was, of course, an unavoidable part of the project of peddling concerts, scores, and recordings in a market economy. But it is also an important way in which many individuals define themselves and their tastes as listeners. In the autumn of 1982, Pärt's *tintinnabuli* works were featured in no fewer than three festivals of "minimal" (or minimalist) music—in Paris, Utrecht, and Karlsruhe.[28] In the press, the "minimalist" label cropped up frequently, and some allied his music with the ostensible "new simplicity" (*neue Einfachkeit*) of the West German composers Manfred Trojan and Wolfgang Rihm.[29] Soon these currents of reception would merge with the millennial discourse in Anglophone commentary on the collapse of European communism, giving rise to the "holy minimalism" and "end of history" tropes we saw in chapter 1. Some of the labeling was particularly insidious. For months and even years after he gave the first of his many interviews to the Western press, Pärt and his music continued to be identified not as Estonian or even Soviet, but as Russian.[30] And although some writers in the Cold War West had called him a dissident while he lived in the USSR, an American paper identified him as a "Red composer" in 1984, three years after he had settled in Berlin, and four since he had acquired an Austrian passport.[31]

A more heartening turn came in 1983, when Pärt embarked on what would become a decades-long relationship with

Eicher and ECM. As Pärt recounts, Eicher approached him about a recording project after hearing *Tabula Rasa* broadcast on West German Radio. (The recording Eicher heard was made by Kremer, Grindenko, and Schnittke in Bonn, during their tour of 1977.)[32] Eicher, who founded ECM in 1969 with a focus on avant-garde jazz, had recently helped the pianist Keith Jarrett find an audience as a soloist, and he had scored a substantial crossover hit with Jarrett's 1975 ECM album, *The Köln Concert*. More recently Eicher had produced another record that would likewise become a bestseller in crossover markets: Steve Reich's *Music for 18 Musicians*, recorded in 1977 and released the following year.[33] Widely respected by his collaborators for his obsessive dedication to realizing on disc the visions he shared with the musicians he engaged, Eicher partnered with Pärt, Kremer, and Jarrett in October 1983 to record a version of Pärt's *Fratres* for piano and violin. He paired it with the Bonn recording of *Tabula Rasa* from 1977, along with new, Eicher-produced recordings of *Cantus* and an arrangement of *Fratres* for an ensemble of cellos, and he released the four tracks together on an ECM disc in 1984. Entitled *Tabula Rasa*, it was Pärt's first album produced and sold outside the USSR. It inaugurated a new chapter in the history of the record label as well, officially launching the ECM New Series, with discs dedicated to the music of individual composers rather than performers.[34] As the critic Paul Griffiths writes in notes accompanying the latest edition of ECM's 1984 release, the partnership with Eicher "gave Pärt a forum he could not otherwise have found…. Coming out on ECM, endorsed by Jarrett, Pärt's music found its way to a different audience"—an audience steeped in jazz and other nonclassical repertoires, an audience far larger than what one would expect for classical music in the late twentieth century.[35]

As the Russian musicologist Svetlana Savenko recalls, with Pärt's departure from the USSR his work all but disappeared from that country's officially sanctioned musical life. An essay on *Perpetuum Mobile* by the musicologist Liubov' Berger was pulled from publication immediately following the Pärts' emigration in January 1980, and it remained unprinted until the final days of the Soviet Union itself. By the end of the decade a generation of Soviet composers had come of age never having known Pärt as a living presence. Yet his reputation endured. In his absence—to quote Savenko—he became "a legendary figure."[36] With the advent of glasnost and perestroika, however, Pärt's music began to make its way back onto Soviet concert programs, including one of October 1989 under the auspices of Moscow's *Al'ternativa-?* festival, dedicated entirely to music by composers who had emigrated in the 1970s and '80s. The festival itself, as William Quillen notes, was organized in an attempt "to help fill in 'blank spots' in the concert-going Soviet public's knowledge about twentieth-century music." In this way the festival, and Pärt's *tintinnabuli* works in particular, became emblematic of a broader reassessment of Soviet historical experience and memory.[37]

Tabula Rasa itself figured prominently in another testament to such historical reimagining, the film *Repentance* (in Russian, *Pokaianie*) by the Georgian director Tangiz Abuladze. Shot in 1984 but released only in 1986–87, the movie was a powerful indictment of a culture of unchecked and unfeeling political power, whose narrative and visual allusions to Stalinism escaped the notice of no one. "The breakout hit of perestroika," *Repentance* was seen by thousands, maybe millions of Soviet citizens. One of the film's most famous scenes, the despairing search of a mother and her daughter for traces of their disappeared father and husband, was set to the strains of *Silentium*.[38] In January 1990 Pärt's voice itself returned to Soviet discourse on his music, when a lightly edited translation of an English interview from the previous year was published in *Sovetskaia muzyka*. The following month, Savenko could observe, "Pärt's music is now gradually returning to us."[39]

Even more than the reception of *Tabula Rasa* when it was first performed abroad in 1977, it was the initial response to Pärt's ECM record that set the tone for popular discourse on the composer and his music through the turn of the century. While programs distributed at the 1977 performances provided little if any information about Pärt or his music, reviewers of the record had the benefit of an evocative accompanying essay penned by Wolfgang Sandner, music critic for the *Frankfurter allgemeine Zeitung*. Whereas initial critiques had responded to the tonal stasis, soft dynamics, and generative processes of *Tabula Rasa* in terms of an imaginary "Far Eastern" aesthetic, Sandner reframed those discussions in relation to Pärt's Orthodox Christian faith and often eloquently professed introspection, and also against the backdrop of his earlier modernist creations. Sandner drew attention to the audible traces of histories that permeate Pärt's score (to its polystylism, though he avoided the term), and he closed by highlighting the novelty of the namesake work, in spite of all those resonances. "The tonality of this music," Sandner wrote of *Tabula Rasa*, "has no mechanical purpose. It leads us toward something that has never been heard before."⁴⁰ Sometimes referring directly to Sandner's essay, early responses to Pärt's disc often took up Sandner's metaphors. Herbert Glossner in Hamburg: "Words do not suffice to describe this work, which parts with tonality to venture into enticingly new realms of sound." Peter Rüedi in Zurich: "His music sounds at once completely new and completely old.... His works are devotional objects, they conjure a vanished paradise and awaken mourning for its irrecoverable loss." For Ekkehart Kroher in Munich, the performers on Pärt's ECM disc "make these prayers and landscapes of the soul come alive, this music of stillness born of humility. An anachronism in our noisy, materialistic world? To the contrary: a necessary corrective, worth listening to closely."⁴¹

There was one current of reception from 1977 that still resonated in the 1980s, however. Whereas early listeners had commented admiringly on what they heard as echoes of "highly skilled pop groups" in *Tabula Rasa*, a German magazine reprinted Glossner's 1984 review in its entirety, but under a different title. Originally called "New Music by ECM," Glossner's essay was now headed by the question, "Is 'New Music' Finally Becoming Popular?"⁴² The reference—in German, *Neue Musik*, with the capital N—was to the legacy of Schoenberg's serial music and theories, with which Pärt had first experimented in the 1960s. Such music, Schoenberg had once famously predicted, would someday be embraced by listeners everywhere, becoming, not unlike Pink Floyd, *popular*. With respect to his own compositions, Schoenberg's prophesy had turned out to be flat wrong. But now Pärt's *tintinnabuli* was hailed as a possible vindication of Schoenberg's broader vision. Another German magazine picked up this theme, asking the same question in its own review of Pärt's 1984 disk: "Is New Music Becoming Popular?" On its pages, the critic answered: "The idea of new music is advanced through [Pärt's] music . . . and perhaps loses some of its fright."[43]

In asking these questions and proposing this answer, these writers point to something fundamental about Pärt's contribution with *Tabula Rasa* and his *tintinnabuli* music more generally. For with its algorithmic processes, the rational unfolding of its pitch structures, and its aspects of Cage-like experimentation, *Tabula Rasa* might well be heard as building on important lines of Western avant-garde tradition. But the work's powerful intimations of tonality, its echoes of musics of earlier times, the drama at the end of its first movement, and the fade-like ending of its second all conspire to assure its resonance and comprehensibility among listeners more at home with mainstream classical and even popular musics.[44]

When asked by an interviewer in 1986 about which serialist composers interest him most, Pärt responded: "They don't interest me at all. What does interest me is how they will all come out of this situation."[45] Pärt himself came out of the "situation" of serialism through the same impulse toward ceaseless experimentation that had brought him into it in the first place, and which finally led him into a new tonality—*tintinnabuli*—that he would not otherwise have found. Now, through the experience of his *tintinnabuli* works, countless others have come out of it too, Martynov and his friends among them. At the same time, some of those who were never "in" the serialist fold, who found Pärt's music through popular idioms and other pathways of musical expression and experience, might find themselves being drawn further into classical music more broadly.[46] They might even find themselves drawn to the musics of the postwar avant-garde, having first encountered their sounding traces in Pärt's beautiful art, having there discovered its fascinations, absent disquiet and fright.

ADDITIONAL SOURCES FOR READING AND LISTENING

THE BEST PLACE TO start listening is the composer's 1984 ECM disc, *Arvo Pärt: Tabula Rasa* (ECM New Series 1275). A commemorative reissue of the album from 2010 includes a new essay by the critic Paul Griffiths, photographs, facsimile reproductions of the autograph scores of *Tabula Rasa* and *Cantus in Memory of Benjamin Britten*, and complete typeset scores of *Tabula Rasa, Cantus*, and two versions of *Fratres* (Munich: ECM, and Vienna: Universal Edition).

The most extensive of the composer's many published interviews is found in *Arvo Pärt in Conversation*, edited by Enzo Restagno and translated by Robert Crow (Champaign, IL: Dalkey Archive Press, 2012). The first issue of the journal *Music & Literature: An Arts Magazine* (Fall 2012) includes an additional interview alongside essays, photographs, and facsimile reproductions of pages from Pärt's manuscript notebooks, together with the program notes for the first official concert of Pärt's *tintinnabuli* music (1976), as typeset for a repeat performance in Leningrad the following year. A broad selection of recent scholarship on Pärt's music is provided in *The Cambridge Companion to Arvo Pärt*, edited by Andrew Shenton (Cambridge: Cambridge University Press, 2012). A valuable treatment of Pärt's music in relation to his Orthodox faith is given in Peter C. Bouteneff, *Arvo Pärt: Out of Silence* (Yonkers, NY: St. Vladimir's Seminary Press, 2015). An expansive study of Pärt's early years in the Soviet Union, making extensive use of archival documents and recent interviews with Pärt's contemporaries, is Peter J. Schmelz, *Such Freedom, if Only Musical: Unofficial Soviet Music during the Thaw* (Oxford and New York: Oxford University Press, 2009). The best survey of the broader cultural fields in which Pärt's work took shape is provided in Richard Taruskin, *The Oxford History of Western Music*, vol. 5, *Music in the Late Twentieth Century* (Oxford and New York: Oxford University Press, 2010).

Online, the website of the Arvo Pärt Centre in Laulasmaa, Estonia, includes the composer's official biography and discussions of his music by the center's knowledgeable staff, along with statements by the composer and selected essays on his music, many of which were originally published in Estonian (http://www.arvopart.ee/en/).

NOTES

CHAPTER 1

1 Quoted in Hermann Conen, "Weisses Licht," liner notes to *Arvo Pärt: Alina*, ECM New Series CD 1591 (1995). I have translated the quotation from Pärt's original German, rather than reproducing the translation included with the CD.
2 See, for instance, Mark Slobin, *Subcultural Sounds: Micromusics of the West* (Hanover, NH: Wesleyan University Press, 1993); and Tia DeNora, *Music in Everyday Life* (Cambridge: Cambridge University Press, 2000).
3 Paul Hillier, *Arvo Pärt* (Oxford: Oxford University Press, 1997), 17–18.
4 Quoted from *Modern Minimalists with Björk*, part 2 (BBC, 1997), at 0:02:51, accessed January 1, 2017, http://www.youtube.com/watch?v=2QTxvmlA95Q.
5 Alex Ross, "Consolations: The Uncanny Voice of Arvo Pärt," *New Yorker*, December 2, 2002, accessed January 1, 2017, http://www.therestisnoise.com/2004/04/arvo_prt_1.html.
6 Patrick Giles, "Sharps and Flats," *Salon*, November 18, 1999, accessed January 1, 2017, http://www.salon.com/1999/11/18/tabula. Giles writes about Pärt's *Tabula Rasa* record of 1984, confusing the release date of the album with the date of the work's composition.
7 Ross, "Consolations." For more on Pärt's music in relation to tropes of illness, see Maria Cizmic, "Transcending the Icon: Spirituality and Postmodernism in Arvo Pärt's *Tabula Rasa* and *Spiegel im Spiegel*," *Twentieth-Century Music* 5 (2008): 45–78.
8 On such historicism, see Richard Taruskin, *The Oxford History of Western Music* (Oxford and New York: Oxford University Press, 2010), 3:xvi–xx and 3:411–16. In theorizing my formulation I also draw from John Lysaker, "Finding Our Bearings with Art," *Nonsite*, June 22, 2015, accessed January 1, 2017, http://nonsite.org/article/finding-our-bearings-with-art.
9 Pärt's official biography is published on the APC website, accessed January 1, 2017, http://www.arvopart.ee/en/arvo-part-2/biography/long/. The most extensive of his many published interviews are in *Gespräch* and *Conversation*.

10 Oliver Kautny, *Arvo Pärt zwischen Ost und West: Rezeptionsgeschichte* (Stuttgart: J. B. Metzler, 2002).
11 Quoted in an interview with Peter Schmelz in his "Listening, Memory, and the Thaw: Unofficial Music and Society in the Soviet Union, 1956–1974" (Ph.D. diss., University of California, Berkeley, 2002), 524 n. 50 (the brackets are in Schmelz's original). Grindenko recalled the festival as occurring in 1975, but the first such event in Riga was held in April 1976—the month, according to Pärt's records, of the premiere of *Sarah Was Ninety Years Old* in that city (the work was later called *Modus*, then rechristened *Sarah*); see Pärt's unpublished musical diary from April 1976 (notebook 8, p. 9), at APC. The fullest description of the Riga festival is Boriss Avramecs, "Neoficiālie laikmetīgās mūzikas festivāli 1976. un 1977. gados Rīgā" [The unofficial festivals of contemporary music in Riga in 1976 and 1977], in *Robežu pārkāpšana: Mākslu sintēze un paralēles*, ed. Ieva Astahovska (Riga: Laikmetīgas mākslas centrs, 2006), 20–31.
12 Seppo Heikinheimo, "As Kondrashin Defects, an Arvo Pärt Work Is Withdrawn from Tonight's BBC Concert," *Guardian*, December 6, 1978, 10. The concert was announced in the *Times* (London), October 3, 1978, 13. Kondrashin's defection occurred on December 4, two days before the planned concert; see Boris Schwarz, *Music and Musical Life in Soviet Russia*, enlarged ed. (Bloomington: Indiana University Press, 1983), 614.
13 Michael Härting, "Rekonstruktion der Zukunft," *Frankfurter Rundschau*, April 11, 1979, 8. On the festival and its reception in the USSR, see Schwarz, *Music*, 623–26.
14 Anne Rey, "Arvo Pärt, le saint excentrique," *Le Monde*, June 2, 1987, 11; Rey, "L'énigme Arvo Pärt," *Le monde de la musique*, no. 104 (October 1987): 68–69; and Allan Kozinn, "The Mystical Enigma That Is Arvo Part," *New York Times*, March 26, 1989, H25.
15 Arvo Pärt, "Tintinnabuli—Flucht in die freiwillige Armut," in *Sowjetische Musik im Licht der Perestroika*, ed. Hermann Danuser, Hannelore Gerlach, and Jürgen Köchel (Laaber: Laaber-Verlag, 1990), 269–70. On the metaphor see also Pärt, "Aufzeichnungen," *Individualität* 28 (1990): 8.
16 Wolfgang Burde, Editorial, in "Musik in der Sowjetunion," special issue, *Neue Zeitschrift für Musik* 142, no. 2 (March–April 1981): 105.
17 Milan Kundera, "Un occident kidnappé, ou la tragédie de l'Europe centrale," *Le débat*, November 1983, 2–24; Kundera, "A Kidnapped West or Culture Bows Out," *Granta* 11 (1984): 93–123; and Kundera, "The Tragedy of Central Europe," *New York Review of Books*, April 26, 1984, 33–38.
18 Timothy Garton Ash, "Does Central Europe Exist?" *New York Review of Books*, October 9, 1986, 45–52; reprinted in his *The Uses of Adversity: Essays on the Fate of Central Europe* (New York: Vintage, 1990), 179–213.
19 Gidon Kremer, *Zwischen Welten* (Munich: Piper, 2003), 243.
20 Terry Teachout, "Holy Minimalism," *Commentary* 99 (April 1995): 50–53.

21 "Henryk Gorecki," *Guardian*, December 22, 1992, features page, 3.
22 Edward Rothstein, "Mystical, Minimal and Now Onstage," *New York Times*, October 27, 1993, C17.
23 Josiah Fisk, "The New Simplicity: The Music of Górecki, Tavener and Pärt," *Hudson Review* 47 (1994): 394–412.
24 David Clarke, "Parting Glances," *Musical Times* 134 (1993): 680–84.
25 Francis Fukuyama, "The End of History?" *National Interest* 16 (Summer 1989): 4. For a reading of Fukuyama's text in relation to popular music of this time, see Joshua Clover, *1989: Bob Dylan Didn't Have This to Sing About* (Berkeley and Los Angeles: University of California Press, 2009).
26 Alex Ross, "Of Mystics, Minimalists and Musical Miasmas," *New York Times*, November 5, 1993, C32.
27 Edward Pearce, "New Music for Meditation," *Guardian*, December 20, 1992, features page, 16.
28 Uno Soomere, "Simfonizm Arvo Piarta," in *Kompozitory soiuznykh respublik*, vol. 2 (Moscow: Sovetskii Kompozitor, 1977), 212. Important exceptions to this trend in Western commentary are Christopher J. May, "System, Gesture, Rhetoric: Contexts for Rethinking Tintinnabuli in the Music of Arvo Pärt, 1960–1990" (Ph.D. diss., University of Oxford, 2016); and Peter Quinn, "Arvo Pärt: The Making of a Style" (Ph.D. diss., Goldsmiths College, University of London, 2002).
29 Hillier, *Arvo Pärt*, 2.
30 Svetlana Savenko, "Strogii stil' Arvo Piarta," *Sovetskaia muzyka* 1991, no. 10: 19.
31 Quoted in Roman Brotbeck and Roland Wächter, "Lernen, die Stille zu hören: Ein Gespräch mit dem estnischen Komponisten Arvo Pärt," *Neue Zeitschrift für Musik* 151, no. 3 (1988): 14.
32 Svetlana Savenko, "Vozvyshennoe i smirennoe: Arvo Piart; shtrikhi k portretu," *Muzykal'naia zhizn* 2005, no. 10: 19.
33 See Jeffers Engelhardt, "Perspectives on Arvo Pärt after 1980," in *The Cambridge Companion to Arvo Pärt*, ed. Andrew Shenton (Cambridge: Cambridge University Press, 2012), 43–47.
34 The violinist Andres Mustonen, recalling Tallinn's Festival of Old and Contemporary Music of November 1978; quoted in Margarita Katunian, "Unikal'nyi eksperiment so vremenem," *Muzykal'naia akademiia* 1999, no. 3: 2.

CHAPTER 2

1 Quoted in Peter J. Schmelz, *Such Freedom, if Only Musical: Unofficial Music during the Thaw* (Oxford and New York: Oxford University Press, 2009), 333.
2 Schmelz, *Such Freedom*.

3 On socialist realism in music, see Francis Maes, *A History of Russian Music: From Kamarinskaya to Babi Yar*, trans. Arnold J. Pomerans and Erica Pomerans (Berkeley and Los Angeles: University of California Press, 2002), 255–59; and Richard Taruskin, *Defining Russia Musically: Historical and Hermeneutical Essays* (Princeton, NJ: Princeton University Press, 1997), 498–510.
4 Schmelz, *Such Freedom*, 40.
5 See Schmelz, *Such Freedom*, 131–32; Schmelz, "Listening," 115–17; and Schwarz, *Music*, 344–46.
6 Quoted in Rey, "Arvo Pärt," 11.The event Pärt recalls is uncertain. While the most obvious possibility would be the Zagreb Biennale, only one of Pärt's works appears to have been programmed there in the 1960s: *Musica syllabica*, not *Nekrolog*. See Erika Krpan, ed., *Muzički biennale Zagreb, 1961–1991* (Zagreb: Muički informativni centar koncertne direkcije Zagreb, 1991), 31–32 and 227.
7 Kautny, *Arvo Pärt*, 42–43. See also May, "System, Gesture, Rhetoric," 105–6. For more on *Nekrolog*, see Schmelz, "Listening," 118–22; and Hillier, *Arvo Pärt*, 35–38.
8 On relations between the Estonian branch of the Composers' Union and the central organization in Moscow, see Schmelz, "Listening," 116–18.
9 See Schwarz, *Music*, 359–60; and Savenko, "Vozvyshennoe i smirennoe," 17. For a close look at *Stride of the World*, which Pärt later deleted from his catalog, see May, "System, Gesture, Rhetoric," 127–43.
10 Toomas Siitan, "Arvo Piart—pesni izgnannika," *Muzykal'naia akademiia* 1999, no. 10: 188. For more on these works, see Hillier, *Arvo Pärt*, 38–48; May, "System, Gesture, Rhetoric," 113–27; Schmelz, "Listening," 230–46; and Quinn, "Arvo Pärt," 29–34 and 52–59.
11 On Boulez, see Taruskin, *Oxford History*, 5:20–44.
12 Savenko, "Strogii stil' Arvo Piarta," 19.
13 Steve Reich, "Music as a Gradual Process" (1968), in *Writings on Music, 1965–2000*, ed. Paul Hillier (Oxford and New York: Oxford University Press, 2002), 34.
14 Quoted from interviews of 1998–99 in Reich, *Writings*, 235. For further discussion of Reich, Pärt, and "perceptible process," see Quinn, "Arvo Pärt," 96.
15 Kautny, *Arvo Pärt*, 55–57; Schmelz, "Listening," 230–33; "De Harris à Gorecki," *Le Monde*, November 2, 1966; and program from Memphis, Tennessee, February 11–13, 1968, at ETMM (M238:1/4).
16 Quoted in Kautny, *Arvo Pärt*, 56.
17 Marina Nest'eva and Iurii Fortunatov, "Molodezh' ishchet, somnevaetsia, nakhodit," *Sovetskaia muzyka* 1966, no. 3: 20.
18 Schmelz, "Listening," 463.
19 Kautny, *Arvo Pärt*, 63.

20 On Schnittke's debt to Pärt, see Schmelz, *Such Freedom*, 245; and Alexander Ivashkin, *Alfred Schnittke* (London: Phaidon, 1996), 86.
21 Alfred Schnittke, "Polistilisticheskie tendentsii sovremennoi muzyki," in *Besedy s Al′fredom Shnitke*, ed. Aleksandr Ivashkin (Moscow: RIK "Kul′tura," 1994), 143–44. For an alternate translation, see *A Schnittke Reader*, ed. Alexander Ivashkin, trans. John Goodliffe (Bloomington: Indiana University Press, 2002), 87–88.
22 Schnittke, "Polistilisticheskie tendentsii," 145–46; and *Schnittke Reader*, 90.
23 See Schmelz, *Such Freedom*, 295–327. Gidon Kremer, who played in the Tallinn performance, recounts the event in his *Obertöne* (Salzburg and Vienna: Residenz, 1997), 115–17. The composer Boriss Avramecs recalls that closed cities like Gorky, populated largely by scientists and others employed in the defense sector, often had more provocative concert programming than elsewhere in the USSR; see Avramecs, "Neoficiālie laikmetīgās mūzikas festivāli," 22–23.
24 Leo Normet and Artur Vahter, *Soviet Estonian Music* (Tallinn: Eesti Raamat, 1967), 8.
25 See Soomere, "Simfonizm Arvo Piarta," 163. Soomere notes another Warsaw Autumn performance of Pärt's music in 1963, but the festival's index of its historical performances does not mention it. See the website, accessed January 1, 2017, http://warszawska-jesien.art.pl/en/wj2014/0-festiwalu/2135381484.
26 Mikhail Tarakanov, "Novaia zhizn′ staroi formy," *Sovetskaia muzyka* 1968, no. 6: 54–62.
27 Nest′eva and Fortunatov, "Molodezh′," 18.
28 See Schmelz, "Listening," 521–22; all quotations on Op. 17 are from these pages.
29 See Merike Vaitmaa, "Eesti muusika muutumises: viis viimast aastakümmet" [Changes in Estonian music: the last five decades], in *Valgeid laike eesti muusikaloost*, ed. Urve Lippus (Tallinn: Eesti Muusikaakadeemia, 2000), 154, with photographs on 155–73; and Kautny, *Arvo Pärt*, 100–103. On Young's performance, see Taruskin, *Oxford History*, 5:92.
30 On dating the event, see May, "System, Gesture, Rhetoric," 27–28. The quotations are from Kautny, *Arvo Pärt*, 102–3; and Vaitmaa, "Eesti muusika muutumises," 154.
31 Schnittke, "Polistilisticheskie tendentsii," 144; and *Schnittke Reader*, 88.
32 For more on *Credo*, see Hillier, *Arvo Pärt*, 58–63; and Peter Quinn, "Out with the Old and in with the New: Arvo Pärt's *Credo*," *Tempo*, n.s., no. 211 (2000): 16–20.
33 Siitan, "Arvo Piart," 185.
34 On the premiere, see Kautny, *Arvo Pärt*, 85–87.
35 See Kautny, *Arvo Pärt*, 83–97.
36 *Gespräch*, 33; and *Conversation*, 26.
37 *Gespräch*, 33; and *Conversation*, 26.

38 Recorded for the program *Varia* [Everything else], preserved at EFA (filmi nr. 2088). Pärt reflects on the interview of 1968 in *Sacred Music with Simon Russell Beale: Górecki and Pärt* (BBC, 2010), at 0:33:19.

39 Program from Tbilisi, May 15, 1978, at ETMM (M238:1/4); it was performed under the title *Fantaziia C-dur*.

40 Immo Mihkelson, "A Narrow Path to the Truth: Arvo Pärt and the 1960s and 1970s in Soviet Estonia," trans. Triin Vallaste, in *The Cambridge Companion to Arvo Pärt*, ed. Andrew Shenton (Cambridge: Cambridge University Press, 2012), 26.

41 Quoted in Rey, "Arvo Pärt," 11.

42 Savenko, "Vozvyshennoe," 18.

43 *Gespräch*, 34; and *Conversation*, 27.

44 For an overview of *Song to the Beloved*, later deleted from Pärt's catalog, see Soomere, "Simfonizm," 205–12.

45 Of the forty-one film scores Pärt composed in Estonia, as tabulated by Christopher May, twenty-five were completed between 1968 and 1976, when Pärt unveiled his first *tintinnabuli* compositions. See May, "System, Gesture, Rhetoric," Figure 0.ii.

46 On Pärt's path to the Orthodox faith and church, see Peter C. Bouteneff, *Arvo Pärt: Out of Silence* (Yonkers, NY: St. Vladimir's Seminary Press, 2015), 47–50.

CHAPTER 3

1 The pioneering study, originally in German, was Lothar Mattner, "Arvo Pärt: *Tabula Rasa*," *Melos* 2 (1985): 82–99; trans. Isabel Cole in *Music & Literature* 1 (Fall 2012): 29–52.

2 Hillier, *Arvo Pärt*, 86–97. See also Leopold Brauneiss, "Tintinnabuli: An Introduction," in *Conversation*, 107–62; and Brauneiss, "Musical Archetypes: The Basic Elements of the Tintinnabuli Style," trans. Martin Wittenberg, in *The Cambridge Companion to Arvo Pärt*, ed. Andrew Shenton (Cambridge: Cambridge University Press, 2012), 49–72.

3 The differences between the published version and the original are substantial, reaching well beyond orchestration. On these and other versions of the work, see May, "System, Gesture, Rhetoric," 38–95.

4 Elena Tokun, "Tintinnabuli: Stil′ i tekhnika," *Muzykal′naia akademiia* 2007, no. 1: 224.

5 Maria Cizmic, *Performing Pain: Music and Trauma in Eastern Europe* (Oxford and New York: Oxford University Press, 2012), 125–26.

6 Quoted in Saale Kareda, "'Dem Urknall entgegen': Einblick in den Tintinnabuli-Stil von Arvo Pärt," *Kirchenmusikalisches Jahrbuch* 84 (2000): 64.

7 Quoted in Helga de la Motte-Haber, "Klang und Linie als Einheit," in *Controlling Creative Processes in Music*, ed. Reinhard Kopiez and Wolfgang Auhagen (Frankfurt am Main: Peter Lang, 1998), 233.
8 Bouteneff provides a number of possible theological explications for Pärt's metaphor in *Arvo Pärt: Out of Silence*, 184–91.
9 A copy of the program from the concert, from which I quote, is preserved at ETMM (M238:1/4). Notes for the repeat performance in Leningrad on January 27, 1977, are also preserved at ETMM (M238:1/4). For material from notes for the performance at the Festival of Old and Contemporary Music in Tallinn in November 1978, see Tokun, "Tintinnabuli," 223; and Savenko, "Strogii stil' Arvo Piarta," 16. As Christopher May notes (following the journalist Immo Mihkelson), the suite performed on October 27, 1976, was previewed two days earlier in Tartu; see May, "System, Gesture, Rhetoric," 39–40.
10 On Asaf'ev and *intonatsiia*, see Maes, *History of Russian Music*, 257–58. For a complementary reading of Pärt's bell imagery in relation to socialist realism, see Richard Taruskin, *Oxford History*, 5:402.
11 Mahler's letter to Bruno Walter of July 18, 1908, quoted in Henri-Louis de la Grange, *Gustav Mahler*, vol. 4, *A New Life Cut Short, 1907–1911* (Oxford and New York: Oxford University Press, 2008), 215.
12 Jordi Savall, "A Conversation with Arvo Pärt," trans. Taylor Denis-Van Atta and Katherine Linton, *Music & Literature* 1 (Fall 2012): 7–8.
13 Though baptized a Protestant, Pärt recalls not feeling strongly religious until the time of this transitional period. See Bouteneff, *Arvo Pärt*, 48.
14 Siitan, "Laudatio" (2011), published on the APC website, accessed January 1, 2017, http://www.arvopart.ee/en/arvo-part-2/selected-texts/laudatio-by-toomas-siitan/.
15 See Dorian Supin, dir., *Arvo Pärt: 24 Preludes for a Fugue* [documentary film] (F-Seitse, 2001), at 1:24:31; Pärt discusses the notebooks and performs some of their chantlike melodies at 0:38:11. Facsimile reproductions of pages from the notebooks are published in *Music & Literature* 1 (Fall 2012): 22–26; and Bouteneff, *Arvo Pärt* (second and third unnumbered plates after p. 128).
16 Kareda, "Dem Urknall," 59 n. 3. The Pärts supply the corrected date in Bouteneff, *Arvo Pärt*, 178. In Supin, *Arvo Pärt: 24 Preludes for a Fugue*, the composer and his wife and friends locate and discuss the sketch at 0:55:30.
17 On the Third Symphony, see Hillier, *Arvo Pärt*, 68–73; and Taruskin, *Oxford History*, 5:401. For a description of the subsequently withdrawn *Song of the Beloved*, see Soomere, "Simfonizm," 205–12.
18 See *Gespräch*, 39–40, and *Conversation*, 32–33. The metaphor of the "creative workshop" (*tvorcheskaia masterskaia*) is Elena Tokun's; see Tokun, "Tintinnabuli," 230 n. 28.

19 ETMM (M238:1/4); on Hortus Musicus and *Tabula Rasa*, see Reet Kudu, "*Collage* teemal P–Ä–R–T" [*Collage* on the theme of P–Ä–R–T], *Edasi*, November 19, 1978.
20 The performance was eclectic in its instrumentation, however. The climactic point in *Modus*, scored for organ and singer in its published version as *Sarah Was Ninety Years Old*, was performed in the 1976 concert by a singer, electric guitar, and electric bass. The recording is preserved in the radio archive of EPB (ÜPST-2734/KCDR-1020).
21 *Gespräch*, 21–22; and *Conversation*, 15.
22 *Gespräch*, 49; and *Conversation*, 42; quotation on *Summa* from Motte-Haber, "Klang," 229.
23 Quoted in John Rockwell, "In East Europe, Minimalism Meets Mysticism," *New York Times*, July 4, 1993, A24.
24 ETMM (M238:1/4).
25 Program for the premiere of *Tabula Rasa*, September 30, 1977, preserved at ETMM (M238:1/4).
26 Taruskin, *Oxford History*, 5:43–44. All quotations in this paragraph are from these pages.
27 *Gespräch*, 38–39; and *Conversation*, 31.
28 For example, rehearsal number 72, where Pilate sings: "Accipite eum vos, et secundum legem vistram judicate eum" (Take him yourselves and judge him by your own law).
29 Quoted in Brotbeck and Wächter, "Lernen," 15.
30 Taruskin, *Oxford History*, 5:401. See also Joachim Braun, "Zur Hermeneutik der sowjetisch-baltischen Musik," *Zeitschrift für Ostforschung* 1 (1982): 76–93; reprinted in his *Raksti: Mūzika Latvijā*, ed. Mārtiņš Boiko (Riga: Musica Baltica, 2002), 204–26.
31 Aleksei Liubimov, "Vremia radostnykh otkrytii," in *Eti strannye semidesiatye, ili poteria nevinnosti*, ed. Georgii Kizeval′ter (Moscow: Novoe literaturnoe obozrenie, 2010), 157.
32 Urve Lippus, "Modernist Trends in Estonian Musicology in the 1970s–1980s and the Study of Folk Melodies," in *Baltic Musics/Baltic Musicologies: The Landscape since 1991*, ed. Kevin C. Karnes and Joachim Braun (London and New York: Routledge, 2009), 91.
33 My discussion of this point is indebted to a suggestion made by Engelhardt in his "Perspectives," 32–33.
34 Philip V. Bohlman, "Ontologies of Music," in *Rethinking Music*, ed. Nicholas Cook and Mark Everist (Oxford and New York: Oxford University Press, 1999), 22.
35 Kareda, "Dem Urknall," 65.
36 Quoted in Brotbeck and Wächter, "Lernen," 16.

37 A similarly revealing work by Pärt may be his *Variationen zur Gesundung von Arinuschka* (1977), where the M-voice consists solely in ascending and descending A minor and A major scales.
38 Jeffers Engelhardt, *Singing the Right Way: Orthodox Christians and Secular Enchantment in Estonia* (Oxford and New York: Oxford University Press, 2015), 44 and 36. See also Bouteneff, *Arvo Pärt*, 119–22.
39 ETMM (M238:1/4).
40 Introductory comments to Nora Pärt's program notes, published in *Music & Literature* 1 (Fall 2012): 19. This issue of *Music & Literature* includes a facsimile of program notes incorrectly identified as distributed at the 1976 concert. In fact, the notes reproduced in the issue were printed for a concert given by Hortus Musicus in Leningrad on January 27, 1977. Copies of the notes for both events are preserved at ETMM (M238:1/4).
41 Program of May 15, 1978, with Hortus Musicus performing under the auspices of the Estonian Philharmonic; and of December 19, 1978, with Hortus Musicus performing at the Leningrad House of Composers. Both are preserved at ETMM (M238:1/4).
42 *Nõukogude Eesti nr. 20* (Tallinnfilm, 1976), at 0:07:06. A copy is preserved at EFA (filmi nr. 2089) and available through the EFA website, accessed January 1, 2017, http://www.filmi.arhiiv.ee/fis/index.php?act=search_detail&a_id=5796&isik=&autor=&esitaja=&string=n%C3%B5ukogude+eesti+nr.20&pealk=&mark=&mod=3&lang=en&nocache=1369128246.
43 Immo Mihkelson, "The Cradle of Tintinnabuli: 35 Years since the Historic Concert," trans. Robin Hazlehurst, *Music & Literature* 1 (Fall 2012): 15. Mustonen's recollection and the figure for anticipated attendance, originally given by Merike Vaitmaa, are in Kautny, *Arvo Pärt*, 118.
44 Quoted in Kautny, *Arvo Pärt*, 118.
45 *Gespräch*, 45; and *Conversation*, 37–38.
46 *Gespräch*, 56; and *Conversation*, 49.
47 *Gespräch*, 57; and *Conversation*, 50.
48 See Ines Rannap, "Muusikasündmus TPI aulas" [Music event in the TPI auditorium], *Sirp ja Vasar*, October 21, 1977, 10. I also draw on recollections of the premiere by Toomas Siitan (personal communication, December 2, 2014).

CHAPTER 4

1 Pärt recalls the commission in *Gespräch*, 61; and *Conversation*, 53–54. For Schnittke's recollection of the commission of his concerto, see *Besedy*, 243–44; and *Schnittke Reader*, 45–46. Schnittke's orchestra includes a harpsichord, which Pärt did not use in *Tabula Rasa*.

2. A manuscript of copy of the soloists' parts for *Ludus*, the first movement of *Tabula Rasa*, dated July 1977, is preserved at ETMM (M238:2/58).
3. Kremer, *Obertöne*, 129–30.
4. Elena Dvoskina, "Tat'iana Grindenko: novyi put'," *Muzykal'naia akademiia* 2003, no. 2: 51 (ellipses in original).
5. *Gespräch*, 61; and *Conversation*, 54.
6. Mattner, "Arvo Pärt," 89; and Mattner, trans. Cole, *Music & Literature*, 37.
7. Savenko, "Strogii stil' Arvo Piarta," 17.
8. The first line is quoted in Martin Elste, "An Interview with Arvo Pärt," *Fanfare* 11, no. 4 (1988): 337; the second is from Pärt, "Aufzeichnungen," *Individualität* 28 (1990): 7.
9. Quoted in Ulrich Mosch, "Tönende Stille—stilles Tönen: Zur Musik von Arvo Pärt," *Positionen: Beiträge zur neuen Musik*, no. 10 (1992): 18.
10. Bouteneff, *Arvo Pärt*, 121 n. 101.
11. Engelhardt, *Singing the Right Way*, 44.
12. Bouteneff, *Arvo Pärt*, 119 and 122.
13. On Cage's presence in Soviet musicological discourse and concert life of the period, see William Norbert Quillen, "After the End: New Music in Russia from *Perestroika* to the Present" (Ph.D. diss., University of California, Berkeley, 2010), 7–29; and Schmelz, *Such Freedom*, 44–45 and 295–97. Pärt remarks on his possible familiarity with Cage prior to emigration in Jamie McCarthy, "An Interview with Arvo Pärt," *Musical Times* 130 (1989): 130.
14. Alfred Schnittke, "A New Approach to Composition: The Statistical Method," and "Static Form: A New Conception of Time," in *A Schnittke Reader*, 125–30 and 147–50.
15. Cage, "45' for a Speaker" (1954), in his *Silence: Lectures and Writings* (Hanover, NH: Wesleyan University Press, 1973), 191.
16. Cage, "Experimental Music" (1957), in *Silence*, 8.
17. Cage, "Experimental Music," 10; and "Lecture on Nothing" (1950), in *Silence*, 110.
18. *Gespräch*, 76; and *Conversation*, 68.
19. Thomas Robinson, "Analyzing Pärt," in *The Cambridge Companion to Arvo Pärt*, ed. Andrew Shenton (Cambridge: Cambridge University Press, 2012), 94. An undated sketch from this part of the compositional process is preserved at ETMM (M238:2/58). In the sketch, the initial pitch is G rather than A, and the triadic space of *tintinnabuli* is G minor rather than A minor.
20. On the general trend, see Taruskin, *Oxford History*, 5:26–44 and 61–73. For a classic statement on the project of serialism consisting in designing "an impersonal mechanism" and "set[ting] it in motion," see Ernst Krenek, "Extents and Limits of Serial Techniques," in *Problems of Modern Music*, ed. Paul Henry Lang (New York: W. W. Norton, 1960), 90.

21 In the program notes for the *tintinnabuli* concert of October 1976, Nora Pärt wrote the following of *Modus*: "The simplicity of construction and the strictness are easily 'read' by the mind. The logic of the process [*logika protsessa*] is on full display, as it were." A copy of the program is preserved at ETMM (M238:1/4).
22 Reich, "Music as a Gradual Process," 34.
23 Reich, "Music as a Gradual Process," 35.
24 Reich, "Music as a Gradual Process," 36 (italics in original). On Reich, Cage, and process, see Taruskin, *Oxford History*, 5:368–88.
25 Giles, "Sharps & Flats."
26 Jerrold Levinson, *Music in the Moment* (Ithaca, NY: Cornell University Press, 1997), 25.
27 Levinson, *Music*, 15–16.
28 *Gespräch*, 46; and *Conversation*, 39. The technique is also called metrical or prolation canon.
29 On Cage-inspired notions of experimental music, see Michael Nyman, *Experimental Music: Cage and Beyond* (Cambridge: Cambridge University Press, 1999).
30 Reich, "It's Gonna Rain" (1965), in his *Writings*, 20.
31 Friedrich Kittler, *Gramophone, Film, Typewriter*, trans. and with an introduction by Geoffrey Winthrop-Young and Michael Wutz (Stanford, CA: Stanford University Press, 1999), 34–36. See also Jonathan Sterne, *The Audible Past: Cultural Origins of Sound Reproduction* (Durham, NC: Duke University Press, 2003), 266–69.
32 Brian Eno, "The Studio as a Compositional Tool" (1979), *Down Beat*, July 1983, 57.
33 See *Gespräch*, 27; and *Conversation*, 20–21.
34 See *Gespräch*, 29–30; and *Conversation*, 22–23.
35 *Brillianty dlia diktatury proletariata* (Tallinnfilm, 1975), at 0:16:21. A copy is preserved at EFA (filmi nr. 5927). Connections between Pärt's film music and his concert works were first suggested by the German musicologist Fred Prieberg in 1963. See Prieberg, "Die neue Musik in der Sowjetunion," *Die Zeit*, April 12, 1963. The most detailed consideration of this subject is May, "System, Gesture, Rhetoric," 86–91 and 143–58.
36 *Värvilised unenäod* (Tallinnfilm, 1974), at 0:03:20, 0:09:59, and 0:27:30. A copy is preserved at EFA (filmi nr. 5173). A manuscript score for the material related to *Modus* (called *Matus* in the manuscript, "funeral" or "burial" in Estonian) is preserved at ETMM (M238:2/38). Some of the music for the film can be heard in the short documentary *Kaadris: Värvilised unenäod* [The scene: *Colorful Dreams*] (EPB, in 2011), accessed January 1, 2017, https://www.youtube.com/watch?v=ohQYMai64iY.

37 Brauneiss, "Musical Archetypes," 69. See also Cizmic, "Transcending the Icon," 62.
38 Kittler, *Gramophone*, 3, 21–22, and 34–35.
39 Sterne, *Audible Past*, 287.
40 Ross, "Consolations,"; Ross, "Of Mystics."
41 "A. Pärt—*Tabula Rasa*," *Ruch muzyczny*, November 19, 1978 (quoted from a German typescript at APC).
42 Tim Page, "Music: Philharmonic in Program of New Works," *New York Times*, June 1, 1986, 61; Wolfgang Sandner, "Der stille Ton: Arvo Pärt: Ein Komponist aus Estland," *Frankfurter allgemeine Zeitung*, September 1, 1984 (clipping at APC).
43 Susan Bradshaw, "Arvo Paart" [sic], *Contact: A Journal of Contemporary Music* 26 (Spring 1983): 26.
44 Schnittke, "Polistilisticheskie tendentsii," 143–44; and *Schnittke Reader*, 87–88.
45 Schnittke, "Polistilisticheskie tendentsii," 144; and *Schnittke Reader*, 88.
46 Schnittke, "Polistilisticheskie tendentsii," 145; and *Schnittke Reader*, 89.
47 *Besedy*, 244; and *Schnittke Reader*, 45. The second quotation is from Taruskin, *Oxford History*, 5:465–66.
48 *Besedy*, 244; and *Schnittke Reader*, 45.
49 *Besedy*, 243; and *Schnittke Reader*, 45 (the latter translation omits Schnittke's passage about "E" and "U").
50 On the Baroque concerto, see Taruskin, *Oxford History*, 2:177–231.
51 Taruskin, *Oxford History*, 2:221.
52 The autograph and sketches are preserved at ETMM (M238:2/8 and M238:2/58). Sketches for the first movement reveal that a cadenza-like conclusion was planned from an early date, but its outlines are only partly evident in the surviving materials.
53 Taruskin, *Oxford History*, 5:466. For a different yet complementary reading of the drama of *Ludus* in relation to Orthodox notions of transcendence, see Cizmic, "Transcending the Icon," 60–63.
54 On the notion of an "imaginary West," see Alexei Yurchak, *Everything Was Forever, Until It Was No More: The Last Soviet Generation* (Princeton, NJ: Princeton University Press, 2006).
55 Brian Eno, "Generating and Organizing Variety in the Arts," *Studio International*, November/December 1976, 282; reprinted as "The Great Learning," in *A Year with Swollen Appendices: Brian Eno's Diary* (London: Faber and Faber, 1996), 340 (italics in original).
56 *Gespräch*, 61–62; and *Conversation*, 54.
57 Aurora Semper, "Rahvusvahelise muusikapäeva tähistamiseks" [In celebration of International Music Days], *Rahva Haal*, October 27, 1977 (clipping at APC).
58 Rannap, "Muusikasündmus TPI aulas," 10. (ellipses and spacing reproduced as in original).

59 Program preserved at ETMM (M238:1/3).
60 Quoted from memory in Kremer, *Zwischen Welten*, 192 (ellipses in original). Kremer identifies the official as Vladimir Popov.

CHAPTER 5

1 Kremer, *Zwischen Welten*, 239.
2 Wolf-Eberhard von Lewinski, *Gidon Kremer: Interviews, Tatsachen, Meinungen* (Mainz: B. Schott's Söhne, 1982), 9–10; and Kremer, *Zwischen Welten*, 193–224.
3 Kremer, *Zwischen Welten*, 238. Kremer recounts the story of the tour on pp. 237–57. Unless otherwise indicated, all information in this paragraph is taken from these pages.
4 Kremer, *Zwischen Welten*, 241.
5 Kremer, *Zwischen Welten*, 269 and 276.
6 Hans G. Schürmann, review, *General-Anzeiger* (Bonn), November 29, 1977 (typescript copy at ETMM, M238:1/20). Programs from Graz, December 12, 1977, and from Leverkusen, November 25, 1977, at ETMM (M238:1/6).
7 Joachim Kaiser, "Zarte, aufregende Abenteuer," *Süddeutsche Zeitung* (Munich), November 21, 1977, 14; Ingeborg Schwenke Runkel, "Paerts 'Silentium'—wie ein Hauch von Ewigkeit," *Kölner Stadt-Anzeiger*, November 29, 1977 (clipping at ETMM, M238:1/20).
8 Schürmann, review; program from Vienna, December 8, 1977, at ETMM (M238:1/6); Rudolf Klein, "Neues aus Wiener Konzertsälen," *Österreichische Musikzeitschrift* 33, no. 1 (1978): 45.
9 Harald Wihler, "Magier mit der Geige: Das 'kleine' Konzert der russischen Gäste," *Bonner Rundschau*, November 29, 1977 (clipping at APC).
10 M. M., "Bis ins letzte ausmusiziert," *Süd-Ost Tagespost* (Graz), December 14, 1977, 9 (I have reversed the order of the critic's clauses).
11 Program from Bonn, November 26, 1977, at ETMM (M238:1/6).
12 Programs at ETMM (M238:1/3): Kiev, November 29, 1977; Riga, January 10, 1978; Leningrad, January 4, 1979; Moscow, January 7, 1979. Program from Kislovodsk, February 25, 1978, at ETMM (M238:1/4).
13 Pärt's award is preserved at ETMM (M238:1/7). Program from Warsaw, September 24, 1978, at ETMM (M238:1/5). Program from Tallinn, November 12, 1978, at ETMM (M238:1/3).
14 Programs at ETMM (M238:1/4): Leningrad Philharmonic, January 27, 1977; Tallinn Philharmonic, May 15, 1978; Leningrad House of Composers, December 19, 1978. On the East German festival, see Martin Schmah, "Sowjetische Musiktage in der DDR," *Musik und Gesellschaft*, January 1977, 20.
15 Vladimir Martynov, "Povorot 1974–1975 godov," in *Eti strannye semidesiatye, ili poteria nevinnosti*, ed. Georgii Kizeval′ter (Moscow: Novoe literaturnoe

obozrenie, 2010), 172; Liubimov, "Vremia radostnykh otkrytii"; and Hardijs Lediņš, "Vai esmu iegājis vēsturē kā mūziķis?" [Have I gone down in history as a musician?], *Padomju jaunatne*, October 21, 1989.

16 Program from Tbilisi, May 15, 1978, at ETMM (M238:1/4).
17 The concert was announced in the *Times* (London), October 3, 1978, 13. Its cancellation was announced in Heikinheimo, "As Kondrashin Defects."
18 Seppo Heikinheimo, "Matkustuskiellon syyt epäselvät; Pärtin poissaolo ei romuta konserttia" [Reasons for the travel ban are unclear; Pärt's absence does not wreck the concert], *Helsingin Sanomat*, August 1, 1979, 18.
19 Quoted in Alan Levy, "Paert [sic]: Music That Roars," *International Herald Tribune*, January 31–February 1, 1981, 7W.
20 Mikhail Rudy, quoted in "Eine Art religiöser Hunger," *Der Spiegel*, October 10, 1977, 169; and Gidon Kremer, quoted in "Man muß als Künstler ein Risiko tragen," *Der Spiegel*, December 17, 1979, 151. On other departures from the USSR, see Schwarz, *Music*, 597–98 and 614–15.
21 Quoted in Rey, "Arvo Pärt," 11. Peter Bouteneff suggests that Pärt's conversion to Orthdoxy might have further complicated his relations with Soviet officials; see Bouteneff, *Arvo Pärt*, 50.
22 Quoted in Rey, "Arvo Pärt," 11.
23 *Gespräch*, 51–54; and *Conversation*, 44–47. Pärt was expelled from the Composers' Union on November 13, 1979; the family left the USSR on January 18, 1980. See Supin, dir., *Arvo Pärt: 24 Preludes for a Fugue*, at 1:22:49 and 1:23:41.
24 *Gespräch*, 55; and *Conversation*, 47.
25 See *Gespräch*, 55; and *Conversation*, 47–48. Pärt had previously published one work with Universal, *Perpetuum Mobile*, in 1968.
26 Franz Endler, "Ein Musiker wartet in Wien," *Die Presse*, January 29, 1980, 5.
27 Program from London, January 28, 1981, at APC. On Continuum's programming, see Harlow Robinson, "The Soviet Avant-Garde," *New York Times*, January 11, 1981, A19.
28 Programs at APC: Karlsruhe, October 18–24, 1982 ("Minimal Music in Europa"); Paris, October 27–30, 1982 ("Aspects de la Musique Minimale"). The performance at Utrecht's Europees Minimal Music Festival was reviewed in Ernst Vermeulen, "Duits ensemble imponeert met componist Pärt" [German ensemble is impressive with composer Pärt], *NRC Handelsblad*, November 22, 1982 (clipping at APC).
29 For instance, Härting, "Rekonstruktion der Zukunft"; Reinhold Urmetzer, "Die Jungen hören zu," *Stuttgarter Zeitung*, October 28, 1982 (clipping at APC); Kees Polling, "Minimal Musik: Niet onder één noemer te vangen" [Minimal music: it can't be reduced to a common denominator], *Muziek en dans*, December 1982, 13–15; Max Nyffeler, "Die alte und die neue Avantgarde," *Frankfurter allgemeine*

Zeitung, March 29, 1979, 21; and "Neue Musik in konzentrierten Streiflichtern," *Neue Zürcher Zeitung*, May 9, 1984 (clipping at APC).

30 Claus Henning Bachmann, "Konstruktiv vermittelte Gefühle: Neue Werke von Sophia Gubaidulina, Alfred Schnittke und Arvo Pärt bei den Berliner Festwochen 1982," *Neue Zeitschrift für Musik* 143, no. 12 (1982): 43–45; and Nicholas Kenyon, "Musical Events," *New Yorker*, February 15, 1982, 120–23.

31 Bill Zakariasen, "Red Composer at Tully Hall," *New York Daily News*, March 12, 1984 (clipping at APC).

32 See *Gespräch*, 59–60; and *Conversation*, 51–52.

33 See Peter Elsdon, *Keith Jarrett's The Köln Concert* (Oxford and New York: Oxford University Press, 2013), 18–19. On the Reich album, see Taruskin, *Oxford History*, 5:387.

34 See Paul Griffiths and Steve Lake, "'We Work in the Dark': An Interview with Manfred Eicher," in *Horizons Touched: The Music of ECM*, ed. Steve Lake and Paul Griffiths (London: Granta Books, 2007), 374.

35 Paul Griffiths, "Now, and Then," liner notes to commemorative reissue, *Arvo Pärt: Tabula Rasa*, ECM New Series CD 1275 (2010), 5.

36 Svetlana Savenko, "Kredo Arvo Piarta," *Muzykal'naia zhizn* 1995, no. 9: 18; and Liubov' Berger, "Arvo Piart, 'Perpetuum mobile' ('Interferentsiia'): khudozhestvennyi obraz i kompozitsionnaia ideia," *Sovetskaia muzyka* 1991, no. 2: 59–63.

37 Quillen, "After the End," 48–49. A classic statement on the "return of history" in late Soviet discourse is David Remnick, *Lenin's Tomb: The Last Days of the Soviet Empire* (New York: Random House, 1993), 36–51.

38 Quoted from Peter Schmelz, "The Full Illusion of Reality: *Repentance*, Polystylism, and the Late Soviet Soundscape," in *Sound, Speech, Music in Soviet and Post-Soviet Cinema*, ed. Lilya Kaganovsky and Masha Salazkina (Bloomington: Indiana University Press, 2014), 247. See also Cizmic, *Performing Pain*, 97–132.

39 Arvo Pärt [Arvo Piart], "Pravda ochen' prosta," *Sovetskaia muzyka* 1990, no. 1: 130–32; and Svetlana Savenko, "Maksimalizm Arvo Piarta," *Rossiiskaia muzykal'naia gazeta* 1990, no. 2: 11.

40 Wolfgang Sandner, liner notes to *Arvo Pärt: Tabula Rasa*, ECM New Series CD 1275 (1984); reprinted in *Tabula Rasa* (commemorative reissue, 2010), 23.

41 Herbert Glossner, "Sensationell: Neue Musik bei ECM," *Deutsches allgemeines Sonntagsblatt*, November 11, 1984 (clipping at APC); Peter Rüedi, "Urworte: Orphisch," *Die Weltwoche*, September 20, 1984 (clipping at APC); and Ekkehart Kroher, "Neue Musik," *Der Musikmarkt*, November 1, 1984 (reprinted in an ECM press release preserved at APC).

42 "*Tabula rasa*: Wird Neue Musik nun endlich populär?" *KlassikAkzente*, January 1985, 5.

43 Gisela Gronemeyer, "Wird neue Musik populär?" *MusikTexte*, October 1984 (clipping at APC).
44 On the embrace of Pärt's work by popular musicians, see Nestor Siim, "Arvo Pärt: 'I Suppose We Secretly Love One Another. It Is Very Beautiful'" (2010), APC website, accessed January 1, 2017, http://www.arvopart.ee/en/arvo-part-2/selected-texts/arvo-part-i-suppose-secretly-we-love/. On the presence of Pärt's music in crossover markets from the 1990s onward, see Laura Dolp, "Arvo Pärt in the Marketplace," in *The Cambridge Companion to Arvo Pärt*, ed. Andrew Shenton (Cambridge: Cambridge University Press, 2012), 177–92.
45 McCarthy, "Interview," 132. The interview took place in 1986 (p. 130).
46 On some of these pathways and their implications for hearing Pärt, see Kaire Maimets-Volt, *Mediating the "Idea of One": Arvo Pärt's Pre-existing Music in Film* (Tallinn: Estonian Academy of Music and Theatre, 2009).

INDEX

Abuladze, Tangiz, 108
Adorno, Theodor, 10
algorithmic design, 22, 25, 47, 50, 53, 72–77, 79, 125n21
Arvo Pärt Centre, 46, 58
Asaf′ev, Boris, 44
atonal music, 10, 32, 33, 42
Austria, 3, 61, 95, 101, 105
avant-garde music, 9, 11, 14, 19, 21–22, 26, 28, 44, 63, 69–70, 73, 81, 91, 101, 111–12

Bach, Johann Sebastian, 27–28, 32–34, 38–41, 53, 56, 91, 93, 96
Barshai, Rudolf, 102
BBC Symphony Orchestra, 5, 105
Beethoven, Ludwig van, 10, 66
Berger, Liubov′, 108
Berlin. *See* East Berlin, West Berlin
Berlin Wall, 7, 9
Björk, 2–3
Bohlman, Philip V., 54
Bonn, 97–99, 107
Boulez, Pierre, 18, 23, 51–52, 73
Bouteneff, Peter C., 70
Brahms, Johannes, 63
Brauneiss, Leopold, 83
Brezhnev, Leonid, 11

Cage, John, 18, 51–52, 70–74, 79, 84–86, 91, 111
canon, 78–79, 87
 See also early music
chant, *see* Gregorian chant
Christianity, 9, 33–34, 71
 See also Orthodox Christianity
Cizmic, Maria, 42
Clarke, David, 10–11
Cold War, 3, 7–12, 18–19, 51–52, 106
Cologne, 5
communism, 10–11, 106
Communist Party, 11, 20, 31–34, 104
Composers' Union. *See* Union of Soviet Composers
Continuum (ensemble), 105
Corelli, Arcangelo, 86–87, 91
Cros, Charles, 83

Demichev, Petr, 97
dissidence, 5, 18–19, 102–3, 106
dodecaphony. *See* serialism
Dufay, Guillaume, 47, 49
Dvoskina, Elena, 63–64

early music, 45–50, 54–55, 79, 99
 See also Gregorian chant

East Berlin, 8
East Germany, 101
ECM Records, 8–9, 99, 106–10
Egorov, Youri, 102
Eicher, Manfred, 99, 106–8
electronics, 79–84, 91
    See also magnetic tape
Eller, Heino, 29–30
Engelhardt, Jeffers, 57, 70
Eno, Brian, 80–82, 92
Estonia, 4–5, 8, 12–14, 20–21, 26, 29–30, 33–35, 54–55
Estonian Radio, 33–36, 81

Frankie Goes to Hollywood, 8
Fukuyama, Francis, 10–12

Garton Ash, Timothy, 8
Georgia, Soviet, 35, 101, 108
Germany, 12, 96
    See also East Germany, West Germany
Giles, Patrick, 2–3, 74–75
glasnost, 29, 108
Glass, Philip 9
Gorbachev, Mikhail, 6
Górecki, Henryk, 9–10
Gould, Glenn, 19
gramophone, 80
Gregorian chant, 36, 45–47, 54, 56–57
Griffiths, Paul, 107
Grindenko, Tatiana, 5, 61–65, 85, 93–94, 95–96, 98, 100, 107, 116n11
Gubaidulina, Sofia, 19, 101
Gutman, Natalia, 105

Hilliard Ensemble, 59
Hillier, Paul, 2–3, 12, 25, 38, 59
Hortus Musicus, 47–50, 56, 58, 79, 101

intonation (*intonatsiia*), 44–45

Jarrett, Keith, 107–8
Järvi, Neeme, 33

Karajan, Herbert von, 96
Kareda, Saale, 47, 55–56
Kautny, Oliver, 4, 20, 33
Khrennikov, Tikhon, 20–21
Khrushchev, Nikita, 18, 20
Kiev, 94, 100
Kittler, Friedrich, 80, 83
Klas, Eri, 62–64, 93, 96
Kogan, Leonid, 105
Kondrashin, Kirill, 5, 102
Kõrver, Boris, 29–30
Kremer, Gidon, 5, 8–9, 61–65, 85, 88, 93–94, 95–98, 100, 102–3, 105, 107
Kundera, Milan, 7–8

Lediņš, Hardijs, 101
Leningrad, 44, 58, 61, 94, 100–1, 113
Levinson, Jerrold, 76–77
Lippus, Urve, 54–55
Lithuanian Chamber Orchestra, 61, 95
Liubimov, Alexei, 54, 100–1
London, 5, 97, 102, 105

magnetic tape, 73–74, 79–83
Mahler, Gustav, 45
Martynov, Vladimir, 101, 111
mathematics, 46, 50–54, 57, 73
Mattner, Lothar, 66–68
medieval music. *See* early music
Mihkelson, Immo, 35, 58
minimalism, 9, 106
    holy, 9–11, 106
    mystical. *See* minimalism, holy
Ministry of Culture, Soviet, 18, 27, 34, 94, 97

Mosch, Ulrich, 69
Moscow, 7, 21, 26, 31, 34, 70, 97, 100, 108
Mozart, Wolfgang Amadeus, 96
Mustonen, Andres, 47–49, 58–59, 79, 100–1

Neoplatonism, 52, 55–57
New York, 6, 32, 84, 105
number. *See* mathematics

Orthodox Christianity, 6, 36, 45–46, 52, 57, 69–70, 109

Paris, 6, 20, 26, 106
Pärt, Arvo, 4–7, 13–14, 35–36, 100–2
   emigration, 37, 52, 103–5, 108
   film music, 36, 46, 81–82, 102
   Soviet reception of, 12–13, 20–21, 26–27, 29–30, 34–35, 92–94, 100–2, 108–9
   RECORDINGS
     Alina, 1
     An den Wassern zu Babel saßen wir un weinten, 59–60
     Tabula Rasa, 8–9, 106–11
   WORKS
     An den Wassern zu Babel saßen wir und weinten, 49–50, 59–60
     Arbos, 51, 78
     Calix, 48, 73, 78
     Cantus in Memory of Benjamin Britten, 5, 78, 102, 107
     Collage über B-A-C-H, 22, 27–28, 91
     Credo, 32–36, 42, 46, 50, 54, 91, 94, 101
     Diagrammid, 22
     Festina Lente, 83
     Fratres, 107
     Für Alina, 47–50, 59
     If Bach Had Kept Bees, 38–42, 48–50, 53, 56, 85
     In Spe, 47–50, 59
     Miserere, 48
     Modus, 48–50, 58, 73, 82, 116n11, 122n20, 125n21, 125n36
     Nekrolog, 20–22, 24
     "Op. 17, " 31
     Our Garden (*Meie aed*), 21, 27, 46
     Pari Intervallo, 48, 50
     Passio, 53, 59
     Perpetuum Mobile, 22–27, 108
     Pro et Contra, 84–85
     Sarah Was Ninety Years Old, 48–50, 116n11, 122n20
     Solfeggio, 24–27, 42, 50, 73
     Song to the Beloved (*Laul armastatule*), 36, 47
     Stride of the World (*Maailma samm*), 21, 27
     Symphony No. 1, 22, 27, 30
     Symphony No. 2, 59
     Symphony No. 3, 36, 47, 58
     Tabula Rasa, 2–3, 22, 25, 27, 29, 47, 50–51, 60
       composition of, 61–62, 72, 126n52
       premiere of, 62–65, 92–94
     "Tintinnabuli" suite, 43–44, 47–50, 58, 61, 101
     Variationen zur Gesundung von Arinuschka, 123n37
   See also tintinnabuli
Pärt, Nora, 35–36, 43–44, 51, 58–59, 64–65, 92, 103–5, 125n21
Pearce, Edward, 11
perestroika, 6, 29, 108–9
phonograph, 80, 83
Pink Floyd, 99, 110
Platonism. *See* Neoplatonism

polystylism, 28–29, 32, 38, 50, 53, 66, 84–86, 91, 109
Popov, Vladimir, 127n60
popular music, 8–9, 92, 99, 110–12
Postnikova, Viktoria, 105
prepared piano, 62, 69–70, 75–77, 79, 84–87
process. *See* algorithmic design
Purcell, Henry, 96

Quillen, William, 108

Rääts, Jaan, 32
Reich, Steve 9, 25, 73–74, 79, 91, 107
religion, 10, 33, 54–55, 121n13
  See also Christianity, Orthodox Christianity
Restagno, Enzo, 59, 71
Rey, Anne, 103
Riga, 5, 63, 70, 94, 100, 116n11
Rihm, Wolfgang, 106s
Robinson, Thomas, 72
Rockwell, John, 51
Ross, Alex, 2–3, 11
Rostropovich, Mstislav, 84–85
Rothstein, Edward, 10–11
Rozhdestvensky, Leonid, 105
Rudy, Mikhail, 102
Russia, 7–8, 14, 26, 102–3

Sandner, Wolfgang, 84–85, 91, 109–10
Savall, Jordi, 45, 52, 54
Savenko, Svetlana, 12–14, 24, 35, 68–69, 108–9
Schmelz, Peter, 17–19, 26–27, 31
Schnittke, Alfred, 19, 28–29, 61–62, 64–66, 70–71, 84–86, 91–93, 95–97, 101, 105, 107
  See also polystylism
Schoenberg, Arnold, 10, 18–22, 51, 110–11

Schubert, Franz, 93, 96
Second World War. *See* World War II
Semper, Johannes, 32
serialism, 12–14, 18–27, 30, 32, 42, 45–47, 50, 73, 101, 110–12
Shostakovich, Dmitri, 96
Siitan, Toomas, 21–22, 33–35, 46
silence, 66–72
socialist realism, 18, 21, 27–29, 44–45, 50
  See also intonation (*intonatsiia*)
Solzhenitsyn, Aleksandr, 51
Sondeckis, Saulius, 61, 95
Soomere, Uno, 12
Sovetskaia muzyka, 13, 19, 26, 30, 109
Soviet Union. *See* USSR
St. Petersburg. *See* Leningrad
Stalin, Josef, 18, 51, 109
Sterne, Jonathan, 83
Sting, 8
Stravinsky, Igor, 19, 30

Tallinn, 19, 20–21, 26, 29, 31–33, 36, 44, 47–48, 58, 60, 61–62, 92, 100–1, 103–4
Tamberg, Eino, 26
tape. *See* magnetic tape
Taruskin, Richard, 51–52, 54, 87–88
tintinnabuli, 2–3, 5–6, 9, 12–14, 17, 19, 36
  contrapuntal structure of, 38–43, 57
  Pärt's discovery of, 45–53, 55–56, 58
  tonal intimation in, 41–43
Tokun, Elena, 41
tonality, 23, 33, 42–43, 87, 101, 109–10
Trojan, Manfred, 106
twelve-tone music, *see* serialism

Union of Soviet Composers, 18, 20, 29, 31–35, 100, 102, 104
Universal Edition, 105
unofficial music, 17–19, 21
USSR, 3, 5–7, 9, 12–13, 17–18, 29, 33–35, 54–55, 61, 91, 100, 108–9

Vienna, 5, 7, 94, 97, 105
Vivaldi, Antonio, 84–87, 90–91
Volkonsky, Andrei, 19–20

Warsaw Autumn, 30, 84, 100, 119n25
West Berlin, 5, 7, 13, 54
West Germany, 3, 5, 7, 61, 95, 96, 101
World War II, 10, 21

Young, La Monte, 32

Zagreb, 20, 30, 118n6

www.ingramcontent.com/pod-product-compliance
Ingram Content Group UK Ltd.
Pitfield, Milton Keynes, MK11 3LW, UK
UKHW041302180426
11947UKWH00009B/628